PANDEMIC OF LUNACY

PANDEMIC OF LUNACY

How to Think Clearly When
Everyone Around You Seems Crazy

❧

J. BUDZISZEWSKI

CREED &
CULTURE

NASHVILLE, TN

First published 2026 by Creed & Culture Books

Printed in the United States of America

First printing

Hardback ISBN: 9781967613014
E-book ISBN: 9781967613069
Library of Congress Control Number: 2025943473

To my grandfather, who asked the right question

. . . the veil that veils all peoples, the web that is woven over all nations . . .

—Isaiah 25:7

Contents

Part II
Delusions About Politics and Government

Part III
Delusions About Family and Sexuality

Part VI
Delusions About God and Religion

Introduction

Some Crazy Ideas Are Deadly Serious

೪

In reading the history of nations, we find that, like individuals, they have their whims and their peculiarities; their seasons of excitement and recklessness, when they care not what they do. We find that whole communities suddenly fix their minds upon one object, and go mad in its pursuit; that millions of people become simultaneously impressed with one delusion, and run after it, till their attention is caught by some new folly more captivating than the first.[*]

Never has our future been more unpredictable, never have we depended so much on political forces that cannot be trusted to follow the rules of common sense and self-interest—forces that look like sheer insanity, if judged by the standards of other centuries.[†]

We need to face our society's problems cheerfully—but to face them cheerfully we need, above all, to face them.

I think most people know that. When I talk to groups about social topics, I am often asked two questions. "What's wrong with us?" "Why are we going crazy?" The craziness of the culture has become so obvious to everyone in the room that they don't have to explain what they mean. It isn't necessary to go into the details of tampon dispensers in boys' bathrooms.

---

[*] Charles Mackay, *Extraordinary Popular Delusions and the Madness of Crowds* (1841).

[†] Hannah Arendt, *The Origins of Totalitarianism* (1968).

This book is about the first of those two questions: the what, not the why. I think I can help understand our culture's descent into lunacy. I think I can help explain how the descent can happen. I think I can say something about why it spreads and develops so quickly once begun. I think I can even help see through it.

But why is it happening at all? "It's because of P." "It's because of Q." Yes, yes. Any sane and competent thinker can list a dozen contributing causes without breaking a sweat. I've heard them all, from the absence of fathers to the trickle-down influence of the late-medieval philosophy of nominalism. Some of them are mentioned in this book. Yet what caused all those causes, and what made them come together all at once? No one knows that. No one could ever know that.

On the other hand, if we can come to a better understanding of *what is* happening—especially about what is going wrong with the way we think— then maybe we don't need to know the "why." After all, nothing *forces* us to swallow these delusions. Ultimately, we swallow them because we choose to be persuaded by them, even against better arguments. Maybe we can become a little saner. Now there is a happy thought!

People who come to my talks are a self-selected bunch who don't need to be convinced of the lunatic mood of the times. But when I tell friends who are only moderately engaged with social issues some of the things taught in universities like the one where I teach, or which are abroad in elite culture, I get the opposite response. Many respond with disbelief or giggles, or they say, "That's just a passing fad."

It isn't that they've never heard of such ideas, but that they can't imagine that educated people really hold them, much less that they insist on them. *You can't be serious. Nobody can really believe that there are ninety-five genders or that men can get pregnant!*

That's the *wrong* way to be cheerful. Perhaps I shouldn't carp, since I agree that these notions are crackpot. But when people in politics, scholarship, punditry, and everyday life treat "culture wars" as unserious—or as less serious than things like economics and foreign policy—I wonder how serious they are.[1]

Take "gender" again, though gender insanity is merely one of the more bizarre of the many forms of craziness discussed in this book. I agree with the sane majority that not only do we come in two sexes but that deep down every one of us knows it. And yes, I know that some who don't believe in the nonsense about innumerable genders and about people in the wrong bodies pretend that they do. Nonetheless, many of those who press such manias are deadly serious.

I don't mean that they aren't putting over a con. They may be grifters, capitalizing on mania to gain status, wealth, power, and attention—but it's their mania, too. They work desperately to remain in denial, to avoid thinking of the obvious. The exhausting labor of self-deception pushes them into ever more extreme behavior. Just as lies beget lies, self-deceptions beget new self-deceptions.

Moreover, those who press these delusions have with them the universities, school boards, professional and athletic associations, the entertainment industry, many courts and churches, one of the major political parties, part of the other, and most of the media, including most of the social media. Although a barrage of presidential executive orders has weakened their hold over just one domain, federal agencies, these orders have been strongly resisted. Besides, the barrage mostly reversed the previous administration's barrage, and so long as the underlying thinking does not change, a new administration could reverse the reversal. The constituencies of the delusionists are made up largely of people to whom nothing else matters, people who spend their time trying to wear the rest of us down (and often earning a comfortable living at it). Since the rest of us have other things to do, that isn't difficult.

Unfortunately, derangement has real-world consequences. Against everyday delusions, everyday sanity is fighting for life, and the everyday lives of adults and children are increasingly disordered. Our age didn't invent all these lunacies, but in ours they run riot.

Why isn't it serious that we surgically disfigure children and pump them full of hormones to prevent the onset of puberty, then call this "care"? Or that medical journals publish articles discussing whether surgical amputation is the best treatment for people with sound limbs who "identify as paraplegics" or are "distressed" by having all their fingers?[2] Or that "Drag Queen Story Hour" has become an accepted event in numerous public schools and libraries?[3]

Why isn't it serious that so many of us pretend this isn't happening, are afraid to speak up, or think that having a burning concern about it distracts us from more important things? The normalization of disorder and empowerment of lunacy are not to be taken lightly.

But we are not in normal times.

Perhaps to this point, populist readers will have cheered. Now I will lose some of them. Why?

Because the exotic ideas I criticize are not just the fancies of our managerial and opinion-forming classes, as we might like to think. Ordinary people who decry the lunacy of our times often accept humdrum versions of the same delusions, even while denying their implications. We want lunatic premises without lunatic conclusions. We want the poison apple, without the worm. I notice, for example, that moderates and conservatives who protest lunatic versions of "marriage" such as polyamory quite often believe that cohabitation without vows and with freedom to change partners is equivalent to marriage. Again, moderates and conservatives who would consider it totalitarian to forbid women to stay at home to raise their children commonly view women who do choose that way of life as dim bulbs. And vast numbers of moderates and conservatives who find the ideas I criticize crazy *try not to think so* because they have internalized the crazy idea that making any judgment about craziness is intolerant.

This is one of the reasons why insanity can make way so rapidly, for the knife of the premises has already been slipped quietly between our ribs—and we have slipped it there ourselves. And this is why, even though many of the outré symptoms which ordinary people find so ridiculous, offensive, or baffling will eventually fade, the underlying fallacies are likely to outlive them and produce new symptoms, perhaps equally outré. All too often what we mean in calling ourselves "moderate" is that we are only moderately lunatic; all too often what we mean in calling ourselves "conservative" is that although we complain about *new* craziness, we want to conserve the craziness we have swallowed already.

In a bizarre way, some of lunacy's critics tacitly collude with its boosters. For example, many who would agree with the proverb "A bad man cannot be a good statesman" merely accept another form of the same delusion: Your thug is a thug, but mine isn't. Granted, a bad man or a bad woman might sometimes do something good. And rocks may sometimes fall from the sky. But we do not expect to cobble our streets with them.

Tacit collusion is nothing new. The possibility of being committed to beliefs without realizing it has been recognized for centuries. In the 1600s, political philosopher Thomas Hobbes argued that many people who think they believe in God are "atheists by consequence," meaning that they claim God exists, yet embrace premises which imply that He doesn't.[4] Ironically, Hobbes himself seems to have been an atheist by consequence. As a materialist, he believed in something he called "God," but for him it could be only the greatest material body—hardly what has classically been meant by God.

Is all this just lazy self-deception? It is self-deception, but let no one say it is lazy. It takes a lot of work not to think, for the human mind tends to follow the golden path of logical consequences. Eventually, it gets to the end. Once, when I pointed out in a magazine article that the premises which justify abortion also justify infanticide, my editor protested that "people are not that logical." As he said, not many proponents of abortion want to kill born babies too! I see matters differently. People are very logical, but they are logical *slowly*. A conclusion of their premises which they don't accept in their twenties, they may well accept in their forties. Even if they never do, it is likely that their children will.

Already infanticide is sometimes called "after-birth abortion."[5] Remarking that some people consider abortion murder, Bill Maher said on his HBO talk show: "And it kind of is. I'm just okay with that. I am. I mean there's eight billion people in the world. I'm sorry, we won't miss you. That's my position on it."[6]

It's disturbing how quickly we come to take lunacy for granted. There are at least four other reasons why it metastasizes.

The first reason is that the mind which accepts one bad idea can become fertile ground for related bad ideas—even if they don't follow from them logically. For example, a person who has become accustomed to dividing the world into hostile groups according to race may also be congenial to dividing it into hostile groups according to sex, and a person who overrates the importance of having money may be more disposed to think that those who have more of it than he does are keeping him down. Unfortunately, we use certain bad ideas to distract ourselves from the badness of other bad ideas. I may be so sure that all whites are racist that I can no longer think clearly about my own racism, or so convinced that all men are incipient rapists that I can no longer think clearly about sexuality.

The second reason is that bad ideas give rise to such unacceptable results that certain other bad ideas become more attractive than they would have been otherwise. For instance, radical individualism is often thought to produce strong individuals, but it actually produces individuals who are chronically dissatisfied and unable to accept discipline. One of the consequences is the disruption of family life, which disorders children. Another is widespread unrest, dishonesty, irresponsibility, and misconduct. If such effects become unendurable, citizens may begin calling for an excessively strong government to put an end to them. Thus, there can be a strange slide from radical individualism to authoritarianism.

The third is the revenge of conscience, which requires a bit more explanation. If I do something which at some level I know to be dreadfully wrong, I have two choices: Repent, or dig in. Repenting is difficult. Digging in is driven by powerful psychological needs not to believe myself capable of what conscience tells me I have done. For example, if I have treated you very badly but I refuse to be sorry, then to silence the voice of my conscience I may try to persuade myself that you deserved the way I treated you. But in that case, I am very likely to do terrible wrong to you again.[7]

The fourth, which makes clear thinking cruelly hard, is that every mistaken idea—even the craziest—has some grain of truth which makes it seem plausible. For example, unlimited wealth doesn't make people happy, but many believe it does just because utter destitution and squalor obviously make people *unhappy*. Actually, suicide rates are high among the poorest, drop in the middle, and rise again among the very rich. But the fact that lies and errors contain truths helps explain why ordinary people who are not at all deranged can come to hold some ideas which are.

Not all slippery slopes are imaginary. And that, perhaps, is the tale of our times. It would be a fallacy to suppose that everyone who has a beer will become an alcoholic, or that anyone who tells a lie will start lying all the time. But it isn't a fallacy to suppose that believing certain things may dispose me to believe certain others, or that pretending to myself that I don't know the wrong of what I did may give me a motive to invent elaborate excuses which also predispose me to further wrong.

Since some of the slopes are greased, we aren't lazily drifting into chaos. In fact, whether we mean to or not, we are propelling ourselves into it. We are entangled in a jungle of confusion, a spiraling vortex of error. Not every kind of conflict and sharp disagreement is bad. The problem isn't that we are "polarized," but that we are crazy.

I hope that by exploring our everyday delusions, this book may make a small contribution toward sunny sanity. True, someone who adopts his crazy views because of irrational motives can't be talked out of them by reasoning. Once upon a time, someone who held very odd ideas about sexuality asked me to explain my reasons for thinking differently about it. Afterward, he told me, "I find everything you've said completely persuasive. I can make no objection to any of it." "Then have you changed your mind?" I asked. "No," he replied.

Yet let us not lose that hope. Shedding more light on things may present to the imagination the winsome possibility of seeing them more clearly. Lunacy has its own gravitational pull, but never underestimate the attraction of a sane state of mind.

Although each fallacy I discuss contributes in some way to our lunacy, some are merely badly and dangerously mistaken. I've grouped the various delusions and very bad errors according to whether they concern morality and happiness, politics and government, family and sexuality, human nature, what is real and unreal, or God and religion. Priority goes to the mistakes which do the most damage, or which metastasize most readily.

Obviously, many follies are left out. Economic delusions like getting something for nothing seem to me to grow mostly from moral and political delusions driven by greediness. Fallacies about beauty, like the idea that the ugly and obscene are just "another aesthetic," seem to me to grow mostly from the fallacy that good and evil are in the eye of the beholder. The notion that compassion is giving people whatever they want seems to me merely another form of thinking that nothing matters but our feelings. Social fallacies like thinking racism can be destroyed only by reverse racism seem to me merely a variation on the idea that we may do evil so that good will come. I talk about all those things already.

A friend wondered whether this book might be read only by those who don't need it. I am a little more upbeat. True, the book may not be very helpful to those who are most deeply ensnared. But I would like to think it may be helpful to those of us who are merely troubled and confused—to those who are in twilight, wondering whether the world is going crazy or they are—to those who have touched the snare but are not yet ensnared—and to those who are beginning to consider getting loose. And there are a *lot* of those.

At one time I was one of them, and shared many of these delusions myself. For that reason, I know it is possible to get loose. And for the same reason, although I think my arguments are correct, I would not dare to offer this book in pride or arrogance. I know myself too well for that—though the knowledge was bought dearly.

This is a short book. If you have finished this introduction, you have already read one of its longest chapters—the average chapter is about the length of the typical op-ed. The book is intended for lay readers. It isn't "lunacy for dummies"—how insulting that would be!—but it also isn't a single evening's reading. It is philosophical in the sense that it aims to elevate common sense, but not in the sense of being aimed at professional philosophers. It doesn't exhaust the possibilities of argument, but it could have been twelve times the length and still not do that. I don't throw out slabs of dripping red meat, but I don't plan to leave you indifferent. Carry on!

Delusions About Virtue and Happiness

One can, without endorsing hypocrisy, observe that we could do with a lot more tribute to virtue.

—Richard John Neuhaus, "Those Victorians"

Lunacy 1

Basic Right and Wrong
Are Vague and Equivocal

❧

We're living in a morally ambiguous world where most of the solutions to life and death problems . . . don't have clear-cut answers. It's really difficult to decide what is the right thing to do.*

Are the fundamentals of right and wrong clear—or are even the moral basics hard to discern? As in the case of every delusion, the idea that morality is vague contains grains of truth. It's true that everyone is imperfect. It's true that in many conflicts there is wrong on both sides. It's true that decisions from whether to take up carpentry, to whether to go to war, can be difficult. But none of that is to the point.

Whether people are thoroughly good, thoroughly depraved, or somewhere between has no bearing on whether I may cheat on the medical exam. The fact that both sides in a conflict may have committed injustices does not imply that here and now, either may commit injustice against the other.

---

*   Barna Donovan, Quoted in Kandra Polatis, "Why Moral Ambiguity Is Popular
    on TV and the Big Screen," *Deseret News* (June 9, 2014), https://www.deseret.
    com/2014/6/9/20542769/why-moral-ambiguity-is-popular-on-tv-and-the-big-screen.

The fact that I may be puzzled about whether to take up carpentry does not suggest there is some mystery about whether I may steal. The fact that I, personally, may find it difficult to decide whether to cheat on my wife does not imply that the question is difficult in itself. And the fact that it may be excruciatingly difficult to *apply* the principles of just war does not imply that the principles themselves are ambiguous. However difficult it may be to avoid unintended harm to noncombatants, the principle that I must never deliberately target them should not require deep thought.

The crux is to distinguish the senses in which morality is difficult from the senses in which it isn't. There are such things as hard cases, but the basics are pretty clear. For example, although there may be some debate about the criteria for determining whether the patient has died, there should be no need to debate about killing him. The vast majority of day-to-day moral decisions are easy. Most reflect Ten Commandments–sorts of things. Must I be faithful to my wife? Yes. May I lie to get my neighbor in trouble? No. Must I treat my parents with respect? Yes. May I cheat them out of their retirement? No. Most other decisions reflect not these ten precepts, but the considerations which underlie them. Given the duty to love my neighbor, should I be courteous to him? Should I avoid not only killing him, but also breaking his leg? Of course.

Why then are we so fond of viewing belief in a real difference between right and wrong as unsophisticated "black-and-white thinking"?

Let's throw one more puzzle into the mix. Those of us who insist most vehemently that there are only shades of gray suddenly become moral absolutists when our own favorite causes are at stake. Let justice be done, though the heavens fall! And therefore in the name of justice, let us burn down neighborhoods and set fire to police stations! For centuries, the concept of justice has been considered straightforward. Justice, said Justinian's *Digests,* is the constant and perpetual will to give each person what is due him.[1] In other words, it means always giving everyone what he deserves, value for value, honor for good, dishonor or punishment for bad. And yet we today treat justice as though it meant getting our way or bringing about the results we want—which can mean anything.

The simplest motive for the popularity of the claim that morality is vague and equivocal is that we are averse to conflict. Considering ourselves confused saves us the trouble of having to tell those who make strange claims that we disagree—especially if they are belligerent about it. However, two other motives for the popularity of the claim are probably stronger, and require more explanation.

The first of these other motives is selective, motivated confusion. We are willing to think clearly about some matters of right and wrong, but we don't want to think clearly all the time, because then we would have to confront what we have done. We are confused about what is right, mostly because we have already done so much that is wrong. This is bogus confusion, a form of self-deception.

I should be faithful to my wife, but if she doesn't love me, then maybe the lady next door is more nearly my wife than my wife is. I shouldn't steal, but taking your property for someone else may be okay if I do it through government. I shouldn't lie to get my neighbor into trouble, but if he's my political opponent then it's all for the greater good. It's wrong to take innocent human life, but unborn babies aren't human yet. Terrorism is wrong, but my terrorists aren't terrorists, they're freedom fighters.

If we think we are exempt from motivated confusion because we don't embrace any of the fallacies just mentioned, we need to look deeper. For example, perhaps only a minority would buy into the notion that one might be more nearly married to someone else than to one's real spouse. But how many of us make excuses for our own sexual misbehavior? The sexual disorder of our society couldn't all be on the part of other people, could it?

To convince ourselves of moral lies, we have to accept bizarre premises without allowing ourselves to think about them too closely. Once we have accepted them, they become premises for further bizarre conclusions. For it is difficult to draw a line and say, "Thus far and no farther: I will myself to be confused about these things but not those." If we will to be confused, then we will be confused. But we may get more confusion than we bargained for.

Finally, confusion is encouraged by the way we teach the young. Our moral pedagogy is itself confused. This isn't entirely innocent; those in a state of motivated confusion are often motivated to pass on their confusion to others. Let's consider this.

The first problem with our moral pedagogy is teaching things in backward order. Any sane teacher advances from the easy and obvious to the difficult. We don't start the young on differential equations, but on two plus two. As their grasp of the simpler mathematical truths becomes firmer, we gradually provide them with the tools and distinctions needed to tackle the more difficult ones. Much of our ethics instruction, though, takes the opposite tack. Instead of first reinforcing the students' grasp of the Ten Commandments and the Golden Rule (which we treat as "religious" and therefore dubious), we present them with so called quandaries, such as, "What if there isn't enough water for everyone on the lifeboat?" And then, instead of providing them with the tools and distinctions necessary to work out what to do, we simply encourage discussion so that they can "clarify their values." If we taught mathematics like that, students would draw the same conclusions about math that they now do about ethics. What is two plus two? "Gee, I don't know. What's two plus two for you?"

Actually, some schools do teach math that way now, and some people do draw such conclusions. "Math is actually not universal," says one math teacher online; "treating it as such upholds white supremacy."[2] His view is held among many professionals, and is promoted by educational bureaucracies. Middle-school teachers in Oregon and in San Mateo County, California, for example, were officially encouraged in 2021 to take a short course, "Pathway to Math Equity," featuring a workbook which branded as "racist" expecting students to show their work and urging them to find the right answer. An associated document stated that "[t]he concept of mathematics being purely objective is unequivocally false, and teaching it is even much less so."[3] Did the bureaucrats suppose that there are no right answers, or that students of minority race cannot be expected to learn calculation, or both? One suspects both.

This incident illustrates a second problem: Because our schools have been ideologically captured, they teach the controversial political views of certain ideological factions as though they were moral basics. Not many students have ever heard the ancient principle that justice is giving each person his due, which really is a moral basic. Instead they are encouraged to argue about so-called "social" justice, which can mean anything you want. Too often these arguments end either in fury or in indifference.

A third problem is that most of what passes for instruction in professional ethics—in medical, business, and law schools, and even the military academies—is really teaching *about* professional ethics. In other words, we don't teach would-be professionals, say, that cheating is wrong; instead we teach theories about what makes wrong things wrong. This is called metaethics. Well, there is a place for metaethics too. But how is it usually taught?

Suppose we said that because, in planning for the future, some people favor astrology, some throwing dice, and some reading entrails, we should therefore strike a "balance" among these three approaches. Foolish, you say? Maybe so, but that's how metaethics courses are usually run. Mutually irreconcilable meta-theories are mined for nice-sounding concepts or ideals such as "justice," "beneficence," and "autonomy." It would be one thing to say that justice, beneficence, and autonomy should always be observed, but instead they are supposed to be "balanced" against each other because they are interpreted as being in conflict. For example, we are told that beneficence may sometimes require injustice. Because this hodgepodge of different theories doesn't require consistency, it provides endless opportunity for evasion. If you don't like what "value" A tells you to do about situation P, you can switch to "value" B. If you don't like what "value" B tells you to do about situation Q, you can switch to "value" C. And if you don't like what "value" C tells you to do about situation R—well, you can switch back to "value" A. We used to call this being unprincipled. Now it's a methodology.

Our education encourages moral confusion in other ways too. Take the way we approach so-called critical thinking. Students are taught, for example, that *argumentum ad populum*, appeal to the opinions of the crowd, is a logical fallacy. Well, it is. From the fact that most people think the moon is made of green cheese, it doesn't follow that the moon is made of green cheese. But it isn't fallacious to appeal to the opinions of the crowd about things that they actually know about. We don't have inside knowledge of the moon's composition, but we do have inside knowledge of whether we may treat people in ways they don't deserve—at some level, everyone really knows that this is wrong. By teaching that all appeal to common opinion is a fallacy and not teaching this distinction, we encourage contempt for common moral sense.

Or take the fact that we place the young in situations where they socialize each other. Children and teens should be imitative. It's built into the human developmental plan. But they should be imitating their elders, not other children and teens. Peer pressure can be good, but only when it's the right kind of pressure from the right kind of peers. Before the days of warehouse schools and social media, that's how it was. Essentially, we have allowed a good and educational impulse of our nature—natural sociality—to be perverted.

No wonder the young are confused about right and wrong. And no wonder the rest of us are.

Lunacy 2

Basic Right and Wrong
Are Different for Everyone

∽

But after all, what is goodness? Answer that, Alexey. Goodness is one thing with me and another with a Chinaman, so it's relative. Or isn't it? Is it not relative? A treacherous question! You won't laugh if I tell you it's kept me awake for two nights. I only wonder now how people can live and think nothing about it. Vanity.*

The fact that different nations and peoples live differently is hardly a new discovery. Some are polygamous, others monogamous. Some worship many gods, others only the One. Some put murderers to death, others don't. Such differences have been known as long as tribes and societies have had contact with other tribes and societies—in other words, forever.

Today we treat such variations as though they prove that morality itself is different for everyone. What's right or wrong for one person, or for one group of people, may not be right or wrong for another. Logically, this doesn't follow. If every nation practices slavery, it doesn't follow that slavery is right; if some practice it and some don't, it doesn't follow that slavery is wrong for those who don't and right for those who do. That cannibalism has become

---

*   Mitya, in Fyodor Dostoyevsky, *The Brothers Karamazov*, trans. Constance Garnett (1912).

very rare among us isn't just a difference between old times and new ones; it's a genuine moral advance.

On still closer examination, we see that the story about everyone having completely different ways of life is grossly exaggerated. Not all of the variations in practice reflect variations in belief, for no nation entirely lives up to what it professes. Moreover, even the variations in moral belief lie mostly in details. Monogamists and polygamists both believe that marriage is good and that adultery is wrong. Even most polytheists recognize a remote High God, far above the more down-to-earth deities to which they actually offer sacrifice. The practitioners and nonpractitioners of capital punishment both believe that taking innocent life is wrong, wrongdoing should be punished, and graver wrongs should suffer graver punishment.

For these reasons, throughout history the variations in ways of life have not driven most moral thinkers to relativism. Instead, those who reflect seriously on the fact that different peoples live somewhat differently (though not completely differently) have asked, "What are the underlying norms which are imperfectly—if truth be told, sometimes very imperfectly—acknowledged everywhere?"[1]

Well, what are they? In the previous chapter I mentioned Ten Commandments-things. Traditionally, these ten precepts have been considered an excellent summary of the universal norms. Normally they are taken as "metonyms" or placeholders. For example, the prohibition of murder represents the wrong of all undeserved bodily harm, of which the taking of innocent human life is the most terrible. In the same way, the prohibition of adultery represents the wrong of all sexual impurity, of which unfaithfulness to a spouse is a conspicuously grave example.

Nor are these norms just a "religious thing," for the recognition of norms very similar to the Ten Commandments is hardly restricted to Jews and Christians. "Every culture has a concept of murder," wrote anthropologist Clyde Kluckhohn, "distinguishing this from execution, killing in war, and other 'justifiable homicides.' The notions of incest and other regulations upon sexual behavior, of prohibitions upon untruth under defined circumstances, of restitution and reciprocity, of mutual obligations between parents and children—these and many other moral concepts are altogether universal."[2]

Another anthropologist, John M. Cooper, had previously concluded that the norms recognized everywhere amount to a "universal moral code" that "agrees rather closely with our own Decalogue taken in a strictly literal sense."[3]

These reminders were timely because, during the middle of the twentieth century, a number of well-known anthropologists promoted radical versions of cultural relativism. Since then, anthropologists have learned better. The South Sea Islanders were not really indifferent to sexual restraint, as Margaret Mead had believed, and the Ik of east Africa were not really devoid of all notion of moral duty, as Colin Turnbull had claimed. Quite the contrary. Mead was deceived by her informants and believed what she wanted to believe. The Ik, who were suffering famine, believed strongly in moral duty but were under grave stress and temptation.

The fact that pretty much the same basic moral norms are acknowledged everywhere should not be misunderstood. People try to evade them everywhere, too, and different evasions tend to become common in different cultures. Notoriously, although the ancient Germanic tribes recognized stealing as wrong and punished it severely, they didn't recognize banditry against other tribes as stealing. In fact, as among many New World tribes, they encouraged their young men to prove themselves in raids.[4] We too make excuses for ourselves, although ours are mostly about sex. Since casual sexual intercourse leads to unintended conception, we also cut exceptions for abortion. Having cut exceptions for abortion, we can hardly resist making them for other forms of deliberate killing, such as doctor-assisted suicide, euthanasia, and infanticide—all three of which are becoming much more widespread, though quietly.

Even people whom we rightly consider moral monsters do not have a different moral law; if they did, we could not consider them monsters. Nor are they ignorant of the moral law; rather, they pervert it. The Nazi butchers knew full well that it is wrong to deliberately take innocent human life. Grotesquely, however, they insisted that Jews were not human. Prisoners were driven naked to the barracks through stockades so that they would seem more like animals, "to make it possible for [the guards] to do what they did."[5]

Of course, what is right for you and me can differ in one sense, because duties depend on relationship and status. I should be sexually faithful to my wife, and you should be sexually faithful to yours. You'd better not think you should be sexually faithful to mine! But the duty of faithfulness to *one's own* wife applies to both of us.

Taken to the limit, the idea of a different right and wrong for everyone mutates into the idea that right and wrong don't really exist. As the band Jane's Addiction sings, "Ain't no wrong now, ain't no right / Only pleasure and pain."[6] Most people don't take the idea quite so far—but a good many do. "'Right,'" says one blogger, placing the word in scare quotes, "is whatever is right for an individual based on their unique brain."[7]

Really? Suppose my unique brain gives me a destructive temper. If my violent urges are uncontrollable, we might say I am not responsible for my actions, but will this make violence *right for me*? Suppose my unique brain makes food so overpoweringly attractive to me that I suffer a dangerous tendency to eat myself sick. Which is a better description: that I am just "differently hungered," or that I suffer the misfortune of an urge I should try to resist? Or suppose I am a sociopath who is unable to suffer remorse. Morally indignant at being caught after stealing a car, one young sociopath demanded of the police, "How else was I s'posed to get home, man?"[8] No doubt his brain really did have some special characteristics, but would we say that it was *right for him* to steal a car, even though not right for you or me?

Perhaps some people who speak of different wrongs and rights don't mean what they seem to be saying. For instance, perhaps the blogger whom I quoted was carelessly using the word "right" for what is suggested by prudence rather than what is demanded by moral duty. She may have meant that if I have an artistic temperament but can't understand algebra, then I *ought* to consider going into painting but not engineering. True! But that is not the same kind of "ought." My mathematical incompetence might make it imprudent to seek an engineering degree—and, yes, imprudence is a *kind* of moral fault—but I could make such a mistake without violating any moral duties.

For this reason, I cannot be sure what the blogger has in mind. Usually, though, when we say that right and wrong are different for everyone, our purpose is quite different. We use such statements to shield ourselves when we fear that something about our behavior exposes us to adverse moral judgment.

And yet we don't speak this way to shield ourselves from all kinds of adverse moral judgments. We intone the "different for everyone" mantra to defend against some kinds of accusations, but not against others. I am unlikely to trot out the right-for-me excuse to dodge being criticized for robbery. On the other hand, I am very likely to appeal to it because I don't want to be criticized for unfaithfulness. "Slut shaming" is considered a very bad thing, but no one is criticized for "glutton shaming"—although with the advance of the body positivity movement, perhaps that may change.

The argument of the previous chapter flows right into the one presented here. As we saw then, one of the strongest motives for the claim that morality is vague and equivocal is selective, motivated confusion. Now we see that one of the strongest motives for the claim that morality is different for everyone is selective, motivated defensiveness. For by and large, the areas in which we are most likely to plead "morality is vague" are the very same areas in which we are most likely to plead that morality can be different for different people. They are the areas in which our behavior leaves most to be desired.

We don't do wrong just because we are relativists. We go in for relativism because we do wrong.

Lunacy 3

Sometimes We Just Have
to Do the Wrong Thing

∞

Hence it is necessary for a prince wishing to hold his own to know how to do wrong, and to make use of it or not according to necessity.[*]

We don't need advanced mathematical techniques to walk to the mailbox without falling down—but we do need them to understand how to make catenary bridges that won't fall down. In much the same way, we don't need subtle distinctions to understand why we shouldn't play video games instead of feeding the baby—but we do need a few of them to understand why killing in war can be just, or why, in view of that possibility, it's still wrong to deliberately target noncombatants.

The belief, *sometimes we just have to do the wrong thing*, arises at least partly from failing to make such distinctions. For example, many of my students find it difficult to understand that a terrorist isn't simply a freedom fighter by another name—that the difference between just warfare and terroristic violence is more than merely whose ox is getting gored.

---

[*] Niccolò Machiavelli, *The Prince*, trans. W. K. Marriott (1908).

Doing wrong, of course, is bad enough. Unfortunately, once we have done what we know to be wrong, another terrible process is kicked into motion. We rationalize our guilty behavior in order to quiet our qualms, and once we start doing this, the excuses we make take on lives of their own. We find ourselves defending not only the original dreadful deed, but other wrongs it was no part of our original intention to excuse.

Let's first consider two valid and crucial distinctions, then consider how our excuses can slip from the leash.

The first crucial distinction is between ordinary and intrinsic evils. Consider disappointment, fever, and fatigue. These are merely ordinary evils, and if the reasons are good enough, then deliberately bringing them about is not necessarily wrong. For their own good, children who have misbehaved may have to suffer the disappointment of being grounded. It is sometimes better not to fight a fever too aggressively, because a high temperature is one of the body's defenses against disease. Soldiers in basic training need to be exposed to fatigue in order to learn to keep functioning under adverse conditions. We see, then, that whether an ordinary evil is *wrong to bring about* depends on whether more good than harm is brought about under the given circumstances.

But the wrong of deliberately committing *intrinsically* evil deeds does not depend on weighing harms, and has nothing to do with the circumstances. The most conspicuous example of an intrinsic evil is murder. I must not deliberately take innocent human life for any reason whatsoever. Thus I may not hang an innocent man even to prevent a deadly riot, gun down children in the play yard even to shorten a war, or poison my patients even to end their suffering.

The distinction between ordinary and intrinsic evils is not really difficult, but it seems hard for us to learn. Today, my own country is formally committed to the principle that noncombatants may never be deliberately targeted, but it was not always so. When the Allies firebombed Dresden in World War II, making no distinction between military and civilian targets, the intensity of the resulting firestorm beggared imagination: "People's shoes melted into the hot asphalt of the streets, and the fire moved so swiftly that many were reduced to atoms before they had time to remove their shoes. The fire melted iron and steel, turned stone into powder, and caused trees to explode from the heat of their own resin. People running from the fire could feel its heat through their backs, burning their lungs."[1] Hurricane winds produced by the heat blew fire trucks right off the streets. If ever there was a just cause, then surely defeating the Nazis was one, but noncombatants must not be deliberately targeted even to save other noncombatants, nor innocents to save innocents. This was an act of terror.

Interestingly, the point of Just War Theory is not to lay out conditions under which murder is justified, but to lay out conditions in which war might be waged without murder. Murder includes not all taking of life, but deliberately taking innocent human life—and even taking guilty human life indiscriminately or without public authority. Killing in self-defense is not murder, because my assailant is not innocent. Nor is killing the enemy soldier who is trying to blow up the schoolhouse. It's even possible that neither of them knows what he is doing. My assailant might be hallucinating that I am a dangerous monster; the enemy soldier's superiors may have lied to him about the nature of the war or the target. But each is *materially* guilty (what he intends is wrong), even if he is not *formally* guilty (the wrong is not his intention).

But wait! Can't we ever *permissibly* cause harms to innocents? In fact, isn't causing even deadly harm sometimes permissible? Every time we administer a medicine or perform a surgery, we are incurring the risk of side effects or infections, perhaps even lethal ones. And if causing harm *is* permissible, then why not harm some people for the greater good of others? The bioethicist John Harris is famous for arguing that whenever we could save two or more dying persons by killing a healthy person and harvesting his organs, we really ought to do so. Scholars in the field consider his proposal neither brutal nor extreme, but bold and imaginative. Why not? If we chose our victims through a random method—a survival lottery—then "everyone's chance of living to a ripe old age might be increased"! For those whose skins crawl at such bloody suggestions, Harris suggests "a long period of education or propaganda" to "remove our abhorrence."[2] God save us from that kind of education.

Here is where the second crucial distinction comes in. For good enough reasons, we may sometimes *tolerate* the possibility, or even the certainty, of an intrinsic evil, but we may never *intend* an intrinsic evil. This distinction bears the cumbersome name "Double Effect," because it treats the tolerated and the intended results of our actions differently. Thinkers of the "consequentialist" school of thought, like Harris, consider the distinction meaningless. If something bad happens, what difference does it make whether you intended it or merely tolerated it? Whether you bring about someone's death or merely fail to kill someone else so that he can be cured, either way he's not alive!

But it makes all the difference in the world whether I drive my automobile to work even though there is always some risk of unintentionally hitting someone, and whether I drive it in hopes of running someone down. In both cases the act of driving involves the possibility of death to innocents. But in the former case I am acting permissibly, while in the latter case I am a murderer.

And here is another point. Trying to run down those pedestrians will be just as wrong whether I intend it as an end in itself (for instance, because I hate people or killing amuses me), or as a means to some other end (for instance, because even though I don't want them dead *per se,* decisively doing away with them clears the road so that I can get to work faster). For this reason, the complete expression of the principle I have just stated goes on to say that we may never intend an intrinsic evil *either* as a means to an end *or* as an end in itself.

So, we must distinguish intended from unintended evils. If we were never to tolerate even the possibility of unintended evils, human life would be impossible. It would be wrong to lift a finger, because literally anything we did might have unintended bad consequences. If I say "Hello!" to my friend, I might startle him so that he falls and breaks his neck. If a doctor gives a patient a limited-time prescription for a mild opioid painkiller after surgery, the patient might like the feeling too much and seek the drug illicitly. If a librarian orders a book on toxicology, some Bluebeard might use its information to poison his wife. If a soldier shoots a terrorist to keep him from

18

detonating a grenade in a hospital ward, a ricochet might injure a patient. Shall we conclude that we must not greet our friends, prescribe even moderate doses of painkillers, put books about toxicology in the libraries, or use force against terrorists? No. Risks should not be ignored, but they should be weighed against the loss of other goods.

But considerations like these can never make it right to deliberately commit an intrinsically evil act. It is one thing to greet my friend, another to push him over; one to prescribe a painkiller, another to try getting someone hooked; one to put a book in the library, another to commission murder; one to risk an injury, another to aim at it. One of my former teachers once argued that doing what is wrong is merely a "moral cost" that must occasionally be incurred for the sake of greater good, but no: the whole point of intrinsic evil is that no greater good can offset it.

Conscience accuses us. There is the young woman in class who screamed at me in rage because I had given a one-sentence clinical description of partial-birth abortion. There is the young man, a military veteran, whose voice was cracking and who was at the very edge of hysteria when I explained the just-war principle of never deliberately targeting noncombatants. And there is the young woman who told my friend, her crisis-pregnancy counselor, that she had her second abortion to punish herself for having the first one.

In for a penny, in for a pound: Once we justify intrinsically evil deeds, it is impossible to say, "Thus and no farther." The caress becomes a habit. The normal desire to be just mutates into the dark urge to justify myself. The normal desire for concord with others turns into a compulsion to recruit others to do the same thing. The normal desire to confess is perverted into confessionally themed promotion. The normal desire to pay a price is transformed into a quest for substitute atonement, even repeating the act in order to be burdened with yet another load of guilt. To escape guilt, we seek scapegoats. To prove our deeds were justified, we do worse on the same principles. Whether such motivations operate quietly or vehemently makes little difference.

This is why our choices become less and less attractive, and why more and more of the things that pass under the name of making things better make them inexpressibly worse. We justify burning down neighborhoods "to advance racial justice." We lie about political opponents "because they want to do bad things." We give false testimony "because we just know" the accused person must deserve something bad. We unjustly penalize honest people "just to give others a chance."[3] We "solve the problem" of unwanted children by killing them all, telling ourselves that they aren't living, innocent, or human unless we choose to believe that they are. We slaughter countless numbers so that no one will have a "poorer quality of life."

Flannery O'Connor suggested that the logical outcome of tenderness, when it is detached from the source of tenderness, is terror: "It ends in forced labor camps and the fumes of the gas chamber."[4] If we bear in mind Harris's proposal for something like a survival lottery—killing one randomly chosen healthy person and harvesting his organs whenever at least two sick people could make use of them—then O'Connor's point should be easy to grasp. Indeed, Harris has been called "a kind man," and perhaps, from a consequentialist perspective, he is.[5] But the consequentialist perspective on compassion is cruel.

Whenever we suppress moral knowledge, we end up duller than we had intended. The stickiness of the web of excuses, and the terrible sick solace of having scapegoats, drive us ever closer to our destruction.

How can all this be reversed? I don't know how, but I can suggest a place to start. Let us repent that we ever said in our hearts, "Let us do evil that good will result." Let us resolve never to do it again. Let us seek mercy. And let us believe all the things that have to be believed in order for such a resolution to make sense.

Lunacy 4

There Is No Such Thing as Good Character

❦

Done it ever' time. Then I'd feel bad, an' I'd pray an' pray, but it didn't do no good. . . . The hell with it! There ain't no sin and there ain't no virtue. There's just stuff people do.*

People in every age distinguish good deeds from good character, rules from virtues. Even a coward might sometimes master his fear; in fact, this is how courage develops, slowly and painfully, because repeated acts become habitual. Even a fairly honest person might slip and tell a lie; if he slips often enough, the slip becomes habitual, and he is no longer even fairly honest. Most of us work at avoiding that. We admire virtue, desire to have it, and aren't pleased if we think we don't.

For most of us, a model of virtue is the Good Samaritan, someone who gave assistance to a stranger who sorely needed it, at significant cost to himself, even after several people who might have been thought to have a greater duty to help passed by the sufferer. But what if nobody is really good,

---

* Jim Casy, in John Steinbeck, *The Grapes of Wrath* (1939).

21

and the Samaritan wasn't either? What if that time he relieved suffering, but another time might have turned a blind eye? Maybe even Caligula acted kindly at times. Maybe even Mother Teresa sometimes didn't.

Whether or not virtue is real, the thought that it isn't can be pleasing. For one thing, it reassures venal people that venality is okay; as one famous grafter put it, "I seen my opportunities and I took 'em."[1] It gratifies misanthropes, by confirming their dim view of their neighbors, and cynics, who find their neighbors' vices diverting. It flatters the pride of those who like to construct elaborate systems of surveillance, compliance, and control, for if it is true, then nobody can be counted on to do the right thing without being watched and manipulated. It also fits into the postmodern view that there is no *self* but only a string of selves—that each time you do something, the *you* that did it is annihilated just by having done it and another *you* takes its place. Abandon continuity, you who enter here.

On the other hand, everyday life constantly reminds us of differences in moral character. I can loan my car to my daughter-in-law, but had better not loan money to my brother-in-law. The reality of stable character is also confirmed by the experience of banks, insurance companies, and law enforcement. That's why we have credit records, actuarial scores, and rap sheets. These are excellent *prima facie* reasons to think that moral character exists and matters greatly. I advised my daughters, "Marry a man who will be faithful." I did not say, "Never mind whether he's a louse, dear, because nobody has virtue."

Some say belief in moral character is merely an "attribution fallacy." I might think the knife has malice because it cut me; so might I think someone has kindness because he was kind to me. But though careless people do leap to conclusions about others, in fact we see that some people act kindly in a variety of circumstances, toward a variety of people, even when no one is watching. And others don't.

Other people say belief in moral character is just a "folk psychology," like the folk astronomy which says the moon is made of cheese. Today we have better astronomy and better psychology. Hold on! We don't have inside knowledge of the moon's composition, but we do have inside knowledge of

personality. For instance, we *experience* the fact that telling the truth is difficult, but gets easier with practice. Casual disregard of the common sense of
the whole human race should be viewed more warily.

Casual disregard like what? I have been teaching the classical doctrine
of the virtues for a half century. Pushback sometimes comes from students
who tell me that virtue is nonexistent, like ghosts and unicorns. How do they
know? Because that's what some of their psychology professors tell them.

After a certain number told me this, I did some digging. Some psychologists really do propound such a theory. It's a convenient excuse if one is
considering kicking the dog, cheating on the test, or flipping off the driver in
the next lane. But there is much less to it than meets the eye.

Though the experiments on which these psychologists base their hypothesis are somewhat interesting, what they show is another question. In the
first and most famous, by John M. Darley and C. Daniel Batson, seminary
students were recruited under the pretext of having them give talks on either
seminary employment or the Good Samaritan.[2] The researchers had them
fill out personality questionnaires that included questions about their views
and attitudes toward religion. Under another pretext, they were asked to
walk to a different building. Some were told to hurry, some weren't. Each
student passed a confederate of the experimenters, slumped in an alleyway,
who moaned and gave a few coughs. The question was: Would the passersby
stop to give assistance?

Most of the seminarians who were *not* in a hurry stopped. Some were
so eager to help that the person feigning distress had a difficult time getting
them to leave before another seminarian came along. But of the seminarians
who *were* in a hurry, most kept going, and there was little correlation between
whether they stopped and what they had said in their questionnaires. There's
the kicker: From the low correlation (in this and similar experiments), "situ-
ationist" scholars conclude that morally irrelevant situational factors like
being in a hurry matter far more than supposed virtue in determining actual
behavior—so stable moral character is a myth.[3]

Surprisingly, Darley and Batson themselves did not draw such a silly
conclusion. Their discussion of what their experiment meant was much more

thoughtful. Post-experiment interviews suggested that some of the seminary students may have been torn between stopping to help and continuing on their way to keep their promise to help the experimenter. "And this is often true of people in a hurry," they wrote. "Conflict, rather than callousness, can explain their failure to stop." The literature on such experiments gives this point slight shrift.

But the literature exhibits other blind spots too. First, it overlooks that although being in a hurry did make a difference, it didn't make all the difference. A good many seminarians in a hurry helped; a good many not in a hurry didn't. From a failure to find a complete explanation of the difference in behavior, it doesn't follow that the complete explanation lies in circumstances other than moral character.

The second thing it overlooks is that it's very hard to measure virtue independently of what people actually do. Being in seminary is hardly evidential; one student asked me for a recommendation to seminary just because his dad, a Unitarian minister, made a pretty good income. (The student's other top career choice was restoring vintage cars.) Responses to standard personality questionnaires aren't much help either. In the original Darley and Batson study, the highest correlation was between seminarian behavior and whether seminarians viewed religion as a "quest"—but what does that mean?

Third, virtue comes in degrees, and these are *developmental* degrees. Most of us are sorely challenged by our temptations. We win some, we lose some. Each time we win or lose, it's a little easier or harder to prevail next time. Moreover, we find some situations more trying than others; for example, children tend to be dishonest more often with strangers. So the fact that passersby often fail to help someone they ought to help doesn't mean there is no such thing as virtue, but, at most, that not many passersby have it to the highest degree.

Fourth, "virtue vs. circumstances" is a false alternative, because even highly virtuous people don't always act the same way—and shouldn't. The virtuous course of action may *depend* on circumstances. For example, generosity doesn't always require giving everyone who asks for something what he wants. It depends on who he is and how I know him, why he wants it and what for, and whether it would do him true good rather than just gratifying his desire.

Those who say there is no such thing as virtue do take a stab at this fourth problem. As I mentioned, they argue that the differences in behavior which experimental subjects exhibit depend on *morally irrelevant* circumstances, such as being in a hurry. To accept this argument we would have to overlook Darley and Batson's insight that perhaps this particular circumstance *wasn't* morally irrelevant because of moral conflict. But there are other problems.

For consider that fellow in the alleyway. Were the passersby convinced that his distress was genuine, or did they suspect he was faking? Some people do feign distress. Besides, the fellow *was* faking, and it is unreasonable to assume that passersby wouldn't sense something "off."

Suppose they believed his distress was real. What kind of distress did they think it was? If he had hurt himself falling, then he could probably be helped. If he was drunk or desperate for a fix, then they probably couldn't. If he was agitated because he was high on PCP, it would be dangerous to intervene. In many cities, authorities no longer respond to 911 calls about situations like this. Even people who want to be helpful can't help everyone. We have to make choices.

Did the passersby even notice the fellow? Several of the seminarians obviously did—they stepped *over* him! Most mentioned to the researchers that they wondered whether he *may* have needed help. In many cases, it seems that this thought occurred to them afterward, not at the time. Being oblivious when hurrying is surely a flaw, but it is a different flaw than noticing but not giving a damn.

Not to let the passersby off the hook too easily, suppose we accept the researchers' judgments as to whether they did the virtuous thing. This merely exposes the fifth and greatest problem: Where are these researchers getting these judgments?

This question is crucial, because according to the classical view, every other moral virtue hinges on the virtue of practical wisdom, which involves judging well. For example, I may have a perfect readiness to be generous—and such a disposition is nothing to take lightly—yet I may be a poor judge of who stands in need of my generosity.

Now plainly, the psychologists who say there is no such thing as virtue are confident in the stability of their own moral wisdom. Otherwise, how could they presume to offer any judgments whatsoever about what is morally relevant or irrelevant? And if their entire methodology is predicated upon they themselves having the stable virtue of moral wisdom, then how can they conclude that there is no such thing as stable moral character?

Lunacy 5

Good Character Is
Unnecessary for Well-Being

∾

*The only way to get rid of a temptation is to yield to it. Resist it, and your soul grows sick with longing for the things it has forbidden to itself, with desire for what its monstrous laws have made monstrous and unlawful.**

W hat we believe is often far from what we think we believe. If asked, most people might agree that being good is necessary for being happy, but we *act* as though we think the opposite. Alexander Pope's couplet "Know then this truth (enough for man to know) / Virtue alone is happiness below"strikes us as a sonorous platitude.[1]

The grain of truth in the delusion that good character is unnecessary for happiness is that it isn't *enough* for happiness. Socrates famously taught that even under the cruelest torture, the virtuous man is happy. Most of us consider this view preposterous, and rightly so. But we go further, viewing virtue and happiness as being on rather uneasy terms with each other, and that is not the same.

---

*   Lord Henry, in Oscar Wilde, *The Picture of Dorian Gray* (1891).

27

A fortyish man in an airport expressed to me his envy of his teenage son, who was unburdened with responsibilities, free as a bird, and having a good time. After a law-school talk I gave, one of the faculty said to me in perfect seriousness that if there really were an objective moral law, as I had claimed, "Then there wouldn't be fun any more, would there?" Obviously, virtue interferes with some of kinds of "fun." For example, temperance pushes us away from gluttony, although I am pretty sure gluttony was not the kind of "fun" the professor had in mind. And we do come across scoundrels who seem to be feeling pretty good.

Virtue also gets in the way of what we want. For example, I might want your wife instead of mine, or seek to be admired for qualities I don't really have. Self-respect, habit, and fear of discovery may prevent us from sliding all the way into vice, but even so we mock those who "take virtue too seriously," calling them prudes and Puritans, viewing conscientious folk as dried fruits squeezed of the joy of life. There is some excuse for this attitude, because excessively scrupulous people berate themselves for innocent things. But excessive scrupulosity isn't virtue.

What *is* virtue, then? For that matter, what is happiness? The idea that happiness and virtue are independent depends on one large confusion about what happiness is, and another about what good character is. Let's take these in turn.

In every age people tend to confuse happiness with happy feelings, especially pleasure. This fallacy is almost universal among psychologists. Martin E. P. Seligman, for example, says that the first pillar of positive psychology is the study of "positive emotion."[2]

But no emotion is always good to have, nor any always bad; it depends. For example, although these psychologists classify sexual pleasure as a positive emotion, it would not be a happy thing to pursue it by neglecting one's wife and consorting with prostitutes. They classify disgust as a negative one, yet even they admit that we need and ought to be disgusted by such things as cruelty, dishonesty, and boorishness. But if no emotion is always bad or good, then isn't the very distinction between positive and negative emotions misleading? What we need is to have *appropriate* emotions—the right ones, toward the right persons, in the right ways, on the right occasions, and for the right reasons.

In fact, happiness has classically been viewed not as an emotion but an activity, not as something we are feeling, but something we are doing, the activity of doing and living well. Mortimer Adler made this point by saying that we shouldn't be asking whether we are having a good time, but whether we are having a good life.[3] So let's rethink the views of the father whom I met in the airport and the law professor who buttonholed me after my talk. The father assumed that his son was happier because he had fun with no responsibility, but the young *naturally* look forward to assuming responsibility. Bearing it is the spice and stuff of adulthood, built into a life well lived. If today we resist or regret growing up, we are damaged. The professor assumed that any loss of pleasure is a loss of happiness, but doesn't fun become boring after a while? Would anyone want an eternity in Disney World? Satisfactions can be unsatisfying.

And does getting what we want always turn out well? It would be happier to seek the right things in the right way. The adulterer will never experience the mutual trust of faithful marriage. The man who seeks undeserved admiration will find it tinsel. Far better to have the admirable qualities.

Viewing happiness like this, the virtues contribute to it in at least five ways.

- First, because they direct our emotions appropriately.
- Second, because they help us use good things in ways that actually do us good.
- Third, because they help us bear up under bad fortune.
- Fourth, because they help us to withstand too much *good* fortune.
- Fifth, because the very fabric of happiness is to exercise them.

That fifth point needs a few more words. Consider, for example, my wife, who among her other excellences is an excellent seamstress. But she doesn't exercise her imagination, thoughtfulness, selflessness, taste, and sense of beauty in making clothing *just so that we will have clothing*; we are not too poor to buy it. These qualities are rewarding in themselves. As it turns out, the virtues of prudence, justice, temperance, fortitude, faith, hope, and charity are intrinsic to the practice of living, in much the same way that these qualities of my wife are intrinsic to her practice of the domestic arts.

One of the commonest mistakes about virtue is thinking that it lies in extremes—for instance, that the most perfect generosity would be giving everyone whatever he asks, the most perfect love would be doing every possible good to everyone, and the most perfect courage would be suppressing every fear. To think like this betrays ignorance of the age-old insight that excellence of character lies in a mean. Consider courage, which isn't high spirit and fearlessness *per se*, but habitually having the *right amount* of high spirit and the *right amount* of fear under the circumstances.

Most people realize that habitually having too much fear for the circumstances isn't courage, but cowardice. Surprisingly few, though, recognize that habitually having too little fear for the situation isn't courage, but rashness. Consequently they say that we should avoid having "too much courage," when they ought to say that *perfect* courage avoids being rash. Or instead of saying that too much virtue is bad for you, they say that too little vice is bad for you. For example, some psychologists praise what they call "normal narcissism." What they ought to say is that everyone may need *some* of the qualities that narcissists have *too much* of (such as confidence). Narcissism is a character disorder. It is just as foolish to call appropriate confidence "normal narcissism" as it would be to call courage "normal rashness."

Not every action has a mean. Aristotle, for example, points out that a person shouldn't be praised for committing *just enough* murders or *just enough* adulteries. But in every matter requiring judgment, the mean is what we must find. Confusion about the fact that each virtue lies in a mean leads directly to the delusion that good character is unnecessary for a good life. For an illustration, consider an item published by *Psychology Today*, the sole merit of which seems to be saying out loud the silly things that many people think without saying.[4]

Obviously unacquainted with the doctrine of the mean, despite his psychology doctorate, the author argues that we shouldn't aim at complete virtue, just because he thinks virtue *is* an extreme. "No one's stupid enough to turn all their virtue dials all the way up," he says. "We just talk like we should, and sometimes like we do." For example:

- He denies that we should always practice the virtue of caring, because "[o]ne can't care about everything." Obviously; but if caring is a virtue, then it isn't caring about everything, but caring appropriately, striking the mean. This is why classical virtue thinkers emphasized that although the negative duties, such as "Don't murder," apply in every case, the positive duties, such as "Love your neighbor," require only the attitude of love in every case. They do not require every possible act of love, because that would be impossible. By saying that we do not always have to "care" for others, however, the author seems to imply that not even the attitude of love is necessary.

- He denies that that we should always practice the virtue of honesty, "turned up to the infinity," because "[s]ometimes the kindest way to care for someone is to keep your opinions to yourself." Obviously; but his mistake is that the virtue of honesty doesn't mean telling everyone every truth. It means never telling them lies—never saying what we know to be false with the intent to deceive. By rejecting complete honesty in every dimension, the author implies that we may also lie to them.

- He says that his formative years were spent "maximizing" sincerity, in part "to score with women" because sincerity was fashionable. Now, he says, "If someone accuses me of being insincere, I remember that sometimes being insincere is just how I should steer. It's one of the ways we minimize collisions on the winding roads we share." I take this to mean that before, to score with women, he was truthful about his feelings, but now, to score with them, he lies. No. You don't have to spill every feeling, but don't lie.

If we get happiness wrong and good character wrong, then of course we will think that we can be happy without good character, but virtues are essential ingredients for happiness. They don't, by themselves, guarantee it. If all my friends leave me I will be lonely, if all my health deserts me I will be in discomfort and pain, and if all I have done is spurned as worthless I will sorrow. Virtue cannot cure that. Moreover, even if we have good fortune, we long for something beyond the flawed and incomplete happiness of this life, which virtue alone cannot provide.

But without the virtues, happy feelings are water cast on sand. Without them, our friends, health, and attainments are even more imperiled than they would have been had virtue been ours. Without them, we will not even catch the flawed and imperfect happiness of this life, but only chase mirages. And as to that transcendent something—at least the excellences whet the desire for its glory and nobility.

II

Delusions About Politics and Government

The city comes into existence for the sake of life, but exists for the sake of living well.

—Aristotle, *Politics*

Lunacy 6

There Is No Such
Thing as the Common Good

∞

[Only] the individual ... is capable of experiencing good. ... Let it be asked, is not sunlight a common good? No; persons do not enjoy the benefit by community, but singly. *

Politics is who gets what, when, and how. †

After giving a lecture one day, I was approached by a baffled student who asked what I had meant when I mentioned the "common good." None of her political science teachers had ever mentioned such a thing, and she had never heard of it. All of them had told her that politics is *by definition* a pursuit of private interest. I was stunned.

At first, there do seem to be good reasons to be skeptical of the idea of a "common good." Individual persons have what philosophers call "substantial unity," meaning that they "own" whatever their parts do. If a board is being nailed, we do not say, "The hand attached to Sam is swinging the hammer," but that Sam is swinging the hammer, using his hand to do it.

---

* Isabel Paterson, *The God of the Machine* (1923).

† Popular adaptation of the title of Harold Lasswell's *Politics: Who Gets What, When, How* (1936).

Collectivists think the opposite. They believe the "really real thing" isn't Sam, but the collectivity. They see Sam as part of the state in the same way that Sam's hand is part of Sam—in fact, more so, because ultimately, not even Sam is the owner of his acts. Citizens don't have substantial unity; the state does. In the slogan of Benito Mussolini, "Everything in the State, nothing outside the State, nothing against the State." Ultimately, then, the state itself is swinging the hammer, using Sam to do it!

Collectivism is a bloody delusion. Just as I consider my hand a tool, the collectivist considers individuals as tools. Just as I might amputate a gangrenous limb, the collectivist thinks the state might have to amputate a social class or two. "You can't make an omelette without breaking a few eggs."[1]

In rejecting the collectivist delusion, however, it is easy to swing to the opposite delusion, egotism, which is thinking that because the commonwealth doesn't have *that* kind of unity, it doesn't have *any* kind of unity. From this point of view, just as the state doesn't swing hammers, so in the same way the state doesn't experience good—only individuals do. Some individuals get what they want, some don't. End of story.

But no. There *is* a common good. The grain of truth in the egotism delusion is that only individuals can *experience* good. Its error lies in thinking that individuals cannot enjoy any sort of community in the goods they experience.

We need not be naïve. The concept of the common good is often abused. Consider the COVID-19 pandemic of the early 2020s. Public health is a common good, and some governmental decrees—for example, that infected people quarantine themselves—are obviously necessary. But many other coronavirus dictates seemed impossible to explain in this way. Some did nothing but punish activities the rulers didn't like, such as worship. At one point, authorities in California even tried to prevent people from worshipping outdoors, while simultaneously allowing businesses like massage parlors to stay open. Other rules were devised to shift burdens onto persons whom the rulers considered less worthy of life. New York, New Jersey, Pennsylvania, and Michigan issued orders providing for patients with the virus to be moved to nursing homes, causing a surge of infections and deaths among the elderly.

The governor of New York defended the policy by saying that old people are "going to die" whatever you do.[2]

Then came edicts made by officials who wanted to make a pretense of concern for public health. The mayor of my own city of Austin, Texas, live-streamed a video urging citizens to avoid travel, because "we may have to close things down if we are not careful." He didn't mention that he was streaming the video from Cabo San Lucas, Mexico, where he was on vacation.

So what is the common good? A good may be shared, or common, in different ways and to different degrees. Often people call goods common in the extremely weak sense that they are good for everyone. For example, wealth is called a common good merely because we all have material needs. This is misleading, because I might get more wealth by taking it away from you.

However, goods can be common in stronger ways. First, some goods are common in the sense of excluding competition. Pie doesn't exclude competition; if I have a bigger slice, there is less for you. Literacy does exclude it; my becoming more literate doesn't make you less.

Second, a good may be common in the even stronger sense that no one is *prevented* from enjoying it. The comradeship of a healthy family is a common good in this second sense, though not the comradeship of an unhealthy one that torments some of its members. In itself, a bridge over a river is a common good in this sense, though it wouldn't be if I set up a toll gate and passed only those who paid the toll. Even literacy wouldn't be a common good if I used force to prevent you from learning to read.

Third and still stronger, a good may be common in the sense that if anyone enjoys it, no one even *could* be prevented from enjoying it. National security is a common good in this sense. If invaders are kept out of the country for me, they are also kept out of the country for you.

The strongest sense in which a good can be common is that there couldn't even be a *rational motive* for preventing someone from enjoying it, because I gain even from your having it. Virtue is like that. If you have more than I do, you didn't get it by taking it from me. In fact, not only does your virtue make you a better person, but I am better off just because you are.

One of the reasons for confusion is that whether a good is common or not presents paradoxes in all these senses. For example, we saw that wealth doesn't seem to exclude competition, but this actually depends on social arrangements. If there are ways for us to cooperate so that we both become wealthier without making anyone poorer, then some forms of wealth might be common goods after all.

Another paradox is that the private and the common may be complementary. For example, the institution of *private* property serves the *common* good in a variety of ways. One is that each person takes better care of his own property than of what belongs to everyone at once; another, that responsibility is easier to pinpoint if each person has something of his own to care for; still another, that if each has something of his own, there are fewer quarrels. So even though some may have more or better property, the *institution* of individual ownership can make everyone better off than if everything were owned in common.

Still another paradox is that although you and I can't have rational motives for competition over virtue, we can have *irrational* motives for it. For example, I may envy you for being braver. Moreover, although we can't really compete for courage *per se,* we can compete for the reputation for it.

Any good at all may give rise to competition if we bring in the motive of envy, and this has political repercussions. As we saw earlier, if the country is invaded for anyone, then it is invaded for everyone, so in that sense competition is impossible. Yet although citizens can't be unequally protected from invasion, they can be unequally protected from the burdens of preventing it and the burdens that result from it. For example, they may be unequally likely to be drafted into the army, unequally taxed to pay for it, or dwell unequally close to the places where fighting is likely to occur. Concerning these things, they may well compete, fighting to shift the burdens of conscription, taxation, or location onto others.

The only defense against the paradoxes of envy is for each person to regard all the others as friends, as fellow members of a *partnership* in a virtuous life, one in which each of us can not only flourish, but also contribute to the flourishing of all the others. They are actual friends insofar as they form a community; they are potential friends insofar as they aspire to. The very prevalence of this attitude and of the conditions that make it possible are also common goods.

I am not discussing how to get people to cherish the common good, or suggesting that agreement to do so would solve all problems. But you have to believe that the ideal makes sense before you can take any steps toward the amelioration of our messy reality, just as you have to believe in health to believe in fighting disease.

Ultimately, egotism is irrational. Suppose you counseled a mother that it would be foolish to risk her life by dashing in front of a speeding truck to push her child to safety. Suppose you told her that even though the child's death would sadden her, she could always have another—and besides, if she were crushed to death, then she would be lost to the possibility of happiness. People who say such things have never loved. In the first place, another child is not *this* child. In the second place, the death of the mother's child because of her failure to act would be a greater death to her than her own death would be. As Thomas Aquinas remarks, "Since he who loves another looks upon his friend as another self, he counts his friend's hurt as his own, so that he grieves for his friend's hurt as though he were hurt himself."[3]

We often speak of "looking out for Number One," but the mother no longer experiences herself as Number One. And she is right. To say that we are social beings is in part to say that human experience is open to love—that the good life is only good *for* us when we throw in our lot with others who can enjoy it with us. Whenever individuals bear burdens for others, they do it for love. Friends take risks for their friends, parents for their families, and doctors, soldiers, and policemen for their neighbors. This doesn't mean that individuals are mere tools of the collectivity, because ultimately the common good is for the sake of the *individuals* who constitute a community. What it does mean is that they view each other as friends.

Openness to love is the only satisfying defense against the supposed conflict between private happiness and the common good, the only thing that can convert the common good from an abstraction to a lived reality.

Lunacy 7

We Can Attain the
Common Good without Virtue

❧

They constantly try to escape
From the darkness outside and within
*By dreaming of systems so perfect that no one will need to be good.**

M ost of our ancestors took for granted that it was impossible to main-
tain a decent political order without good moral character on the part
of both citizens and rulers. Some, like "schoolmaster of the republic" John
Witherspoon, a university mentor to several of the Founders, went so far as to
think that we always get the government we deserve.[1] As he put it,

> Nothing is more certain than that a general profligacy and corruption of
> manners make a people ripe for destruction. A good form of government
> may hold the rotten materials together for some time, but beyond a certain
> pitch, even the best constitution will be ineffectual, and slavery must ensue.
> On the other hand, when the manners of a nation are pure . . . , the attempts
> of the most powerful enemies to oppress them are commonly baffled and
> disappointed.[2]

---

* T. S. Eliot, "Choruses from 'The Rock,'" in *Collected Poems, 1909–1962* (1963).

Put another way, it is a fine thing not to be jerked around by tyrants, but if we are jerked around by our own passions and desires, we will fall back under tyranny in short order.

While he strongly agreed about the importance of virtue, Alexander Hamilton thought a sound constitution might enable us to get a *somewhat* better government than we deserve. For though he conceded the importance of wholesome motives among citizens and rulers, Hamilton added that history has shown the need for additional precautions. "This policy of supplying, by opposite and rival interests, the defect of better motives, might be traced through the whole system of human affairs, private as well as public."[3] In their own interests, selfish parties sometimes check and balance other selfish parties to the benefit of all.

The Englishman David Hume was far more sanguine than even the most optimistic Founding Father. He argued that a well-designed regime doesn't need virtue at all:

> I . . . should be sorry to think, that human affairs admit of no greater stability, than what they receive from the casual humors and characters of particular men. . . . All absolute governments must very much depend on the administration; and this is one of the great inconveniences attending that form of government. But a republican and free government would be an obvious absurdity, if the particular checks and controls . . . made it not the interest, even of bad men, to act for the public good.[4]

This low view of virtue went too far for America's Founders. As James Madison declared, "To suppose that any form of government will secure liberty or happiness without any virtue in the people, is a chimerical idea."[5] Yet Hume's is the view in vogue today. We blithely assume that no matter how shabby the character of citizens and statesmen, a well-constructed republic with checks, balances, and elections will get along just fine, cranking out justice and restraining the gravest insults to the common good: "The system works!" Let's consider why even such constitutional devices depend on virtue.

As to checks and balances: To keep the government from doing bad things, the Founders proposed relying not so much on written "don'ts" as on a standoff between opposing selfish groups. Other governments had instituted checks and balances between social classes. The Framers proposed using them between the branches of government itself. It was a daring idea. The aim was not to abolish conflict, but to institutionalize it. We were to rest our hopes for the common good not on getting along, but on fighting fair, for a check is a kind of weapon.

But the idea of a balance based on fighting fair raised a profound question, which the supporters of the new Constitution never answered, or even, so far as I know, addressed. The permissible checks and balances are themselves spelled out in written rules. So if written rules are nothing but "parchment barriers," as James Madison called them, then why shouldn't we pronounce the same damning verdict upon *those* written rules? Aren't the written sentences that spell out the permissible checks and balances also just parchment barriers? What is to prevent a political player from going outside the rules completely, fighting dirty instead of fair, competing with the others by unconstitutional means?

The only possible answer is that the Framers thought they had drawn up such good rules that each political player would find it in his interest to keep playing by them. If he did play by them, he would win some, lose some. If he didn't, he might, conceivably, win everything—but he would be much more likely to *lose* everything. So he would think it more to his advantage to stay within the rules than to venture outside them.

The problem is that this isn't always the case. From time to time, situations arise in which some players think—correctly or incorrectly—that they have less to lose by playing outside the rules than within them. In these cases they do play outside them. Moreover, as birds hide from predators in the flock, they hide their foul play in the party or group, where it is more difficult to discover wrongdoing and more difficult to know who to blame. When this happens, we have a constitutional crisis. As I suggest later, that is what is happening now.[6]

Of course, to defuse constitutional crises, we have other constitutional mechanisms; the failure of certain checks and balances is compensated by other checks and balances. But if they fail too, a constitutional crisis can go on for a long, long time.

If it goes on for too long, then the side that first begins playing dirty may become more and more desperate, partly because it persuades itself that victory is almost within its grasp, partly because the consequences of losing now would be unthinkable. Consequently, it throws caution to the winds, violating the rules more and more gravely and openly.

The more it does so, the more frantic and furious the other side may also become, so that it begins to wonder whether it ought to play dirtier too. Once it reaches that conclusion, both sides come unhinged, losing even what little was left of their principles.

So, just as the Founders thought, although checks and balances may make the attainment of the common good *somewhat less* reliant on restraint, dedication to justice, and the other elements of good character, they can't possibly eliminate the need for them. In fact, without a minimum of good character, checks and balances won't properly work.

Now as to elections: Today's political scientists tend to think of elections as ways of amalgamating the policy preferences of a multitude of people. By contrast, James Madison, principal architect of the Constitution, wasn't interested in aggregating policy preferences at all, because he didn't think most people had enough knowledge and virtue to have wise ones. Rather he saw going to the polls as a filter that, if designed just right, would pass through the few people who do have enough knowledge and virtue to have wise policy preferences, and, with luck, get them into the legislature. He took this view because he believed most citizens to be better judges of those who want to make laws than they were of what laws should be made.

He and the other Founders weren't so naïve as to think voters would always vote virtuously. In fact, Madison warned against "the vicious arts by which elections are too often carried," such as bribery. Though he knew that voters sometimes yielded to bribes, he thought they would also recognize and admire good character. Consequently, when nobody was bribing them, most voters would vote for the wisest and most virtuous candidates they could find. To keep corruption to a minimum, Madison relied on the expedient of making electoral districts so large that bribing everyone at once would be too expensive. Since the votes of the citizens would be "free," meaning uncorrupted, they would "be more likely to center in men who possess the most attractive merit and the most diffusive and established characters."[7]

This device has two great drawbacks. The first is that the technology of bribes has outdistanced it. In Madison's day, a candidate had to pay bribes to voters one at a time, *before* the election, each bribe coming out of his own personal fortune. Today a candidate offers bribes to entire industries and social classes at once, paying them off *after* the election, through subsidies, guarantees, transfer payments, and changes in the tax law.

The second drawback is that although voters above a certain threshold of moral and practical judgment prefer candidates who are better than themselves, voters below that threshold don't. They instead prefer rulers *as bad or worse* than themselves. A young man was caught on video camera by a roving reporter after the Monica Lewinsky scandal broke during year five of the Clinton administration. The reporter asked, "Does the scandal affect your view of the president?" The man replied, "Yeah, it makes me like him more! 'Cause it shows he's just like me."

Voters below the threshold also fall too easily for the view that a bad man can be a good statesman: "He may be a thug, but he's our thug." Of course a bad man may accomplish something that happens to be good. But because his motive is spoiled, you cannot be *confident* he will do the right thing; he will do even good things in evil ways; he will be unable to *keep* from doing certain bad things, such as injuring others by example; and whatever he does, he will lie about it.

Eventually citizens lose the ability to recognize bad men as bad men. They view them as strong, because they are bullies, or as smart, because they break the rules. Finally they begin to want a savior: if not a Son of God, then a son of the devil. They hunger for a cure for "this world of troubles," for a machete sharp and heavy enough to cut through the dark vines of the jungle.

So without good character, elections don't work properly, either.

Not even the dirtiest political players want the population to turn against them. Therefore, even the most extreme acts, short of assassination (and perhaps even that), are dressed in the garments of legitimacy. This is an easier set of clothes to put on than one might think, because few citizens understand the Constitution anyway. It is hard enough that checks and balances are so complicated, and therefore confusing. Making matters worse, those who play dirty have a deep stake in making the Constitution as baffling as possible.

It took the Romans years to realize they had lost their republic. By that time they didn't want it any more.

Lunacy 8

The Purpose of Government Is to Take Care of All Our Needs

❧

And I ask the three of you, how can we, as symbolically the children of the future president, expect the two of you, the three of you to meet our needs. . . ? Could we cross our hearts? It sounds silly here but could we make a commitment? You know, we're not under oath at this point but could you make a commitment to the citizens of the U.S. to meet our needs, and we have many. . . ?*

Why isn't the government doing something about that?"
The nonpartisan Pew Research Center reported in 2022 that, despite low levels of trust in government, 53 percent of American adults say the government "should do more to solve problems."[1] That percentage is not much more than a majority, but notice how the question is worded. It doesn't ask *whether* the government's job is "solving problems." The issue is *how much* it should do to solve them. "Doing more" must mean taking on new ones (not doing better with old ones), because the alternative the pollsters offer is that government is "doing too many things better left to businesses and individuals."

---

* Audience question during a debate among presidential candidates George Bush, Ross Perot, and Bill Clinton, October 15, 1992.

That last phrase points up another unquestioned assumption: that the only entities besides government which "do things" are businesses and individuals. What happened to the plethora of other forms of association making up civil society, such as families, friendship groups, trade unions, youth leagues, clubs, cooperatives, civic societies, churches, synagogues, and neighborhoods? So long as we are talking about government, what about the *level* of government? Today, when Americans think "government" they think "Washington," but there is a big difference between wanting the village council to do something and wanting the central government to take it over. Finally, what is meant by "doing things"? It's one thing for the local public school to support parents' moral teaching, and another thing to subvert their teaching by asking six-year-olds what their pronouns are. Yet in both cases the school is "doing" something.

Considering problems or needs one by one, even today most people agree that the government shouldn't try to solve *all* our problems. Yet no one wins election by *not* proposing new laws. Most politicians build their careers on finding things for the government to fix, whether or not they are broken. Once we say the job of the government is to take care of unspecified "needs," it is hard to know where to stop.

Plainly there are some things government must do because nobody else can do them. Yet government is both inefficient, because it has no competition and no profit motive, and dangerous, because it has enormous resources and a monopoly on the legal use of force. Moreover, once something is added to the list of governmental functions, it is extremely difficult to remove it, for it acquires a constituency and becomes a vested interest. Our managerial class is largely a coalition of such interests.

For example, government antipoverty programs seem to have done less to eliminate poverty than to make it more hopeless. They have put food in some mouths and increased family income at the very bottom; these things are good. But they have also created a multi-generational culture of dependency, despondency, family disorder, drug use, and criminality, not to mention petty dishonesty in order to win approval for benefits. The continued popularity of many government programs is mostly due not to the fact that they are helping those they are supposed to help, but to the fact that they provide ever-expanding employment to bureaucrats, and produce a pool of citizens who will vote as desired. Even when a dysfunctional program is supposedly abolished, its dysfunctional activities are commonly only transferred to another agency, where they continue in disguise. A good example is how some welfare programs have been quietly rebranded as disability programs, often with dubious relation to disability.

Those who express such thoughts are often accused of wanting to abandon the poor, but there are better ways of helping the poor than throwing government money at them. Marvin Olasky has documented the lamentable fact that churches and synagogues used to help those in need much more effectively than they usually do today. In the past, the forms of help they gave focused on things they can do that government can't, by emphasizing face-to-face accountability, reconnection with family, integration into the community, and divine grace. Today there is much less of that. Many religious charities see themselves as little brothers of the state, referring people to the government and dispensing *only* material benefits.[2]

Moreover, many forms of association have their own natural callings. Parents, for example, are by nature the proper agencies for raising children. They love them by name, as no functionary does; they can vary their methods according to the needs of each child, something no government or organization can do; and their children love and respect them, not as abstractions but as Mommy and Daddy. Parents have the presumptive right and responsibility to make fundamental decisions about their children's care. Of course there exist unfit and otherwise incapable parents. Thus, in extreme cases, the state may have to step in, even separating children from parents who abuse them or don't care for them. Children may then be placed with others who can be good mothers and fathers to them. Even here, though, the state's goal should be to *support* motherhood and fatherhood, not replace it.

The principle underlying this example may be expressed briefly. Every form of association has tasks to which it is naturally suited, as parents are to raising children, and neighborhoods are to providing friendly support. No task should be shifted to a higher rung on the ladder unless it cannot be done at the lower one. For example, a task shouldn't be bumped from a family to the neighborhood unless the family can't do the job, from a neighborhood to a municipal government unless the neighbors cannot do the job, or from city to state government unless the city cannot do the job. The proper work of those occupying the higher rungs is neither to absorb those occupying the lower rungs, nor to do away with their proper work, but rather to secure the background conditions which enable those on the lower rungs to get on with their own proper work. The most important background condition, which only government can secure, is a just and peaceful public order.

In short: The common good is to be secured not by the government doing everything, but instead by upholding every form of association in its own proper work. Among natural law thinkers, the most common name for this principle is "subsidiarity," from the Latin term *subsidium,* which means "help." Some Protestant thinkers call it "sphere sovereignty," a term borrowed from the Dutch statesman Abraham Kuyper. Still other writers call it "localism," although this can be a little misleading because some functions can be bumped upstairs. How so?

If local government decisions were always made in a participatory fashion, then no doubt it would almost always be better for matters of local concern to be settled at the most local level. The reality, however, is that in all governments—even local ones—decisions tend to be made by elites. So the question is what kind of elites will make them, and whether these elites will themselves respect subsidiarity. Suppose, for example, that the public schools of the city are undermining parental authority by stealthily promoting transgenderism. In a case like this, in which someone on a low level of the ladder is undermining the proper work of someone still further down on the ladder, then those occupying a still higher rung of the ladder may have to intervene. The state government, for example, may have to step in to protect parents against the elites who run their schools.

Federalism—the division of responsibilities between the states and the federal government—is a good example of subsidiarity. It also illustrates one of its practical difficulties. If each state can enact its own policies, then these policies will sometimes vary from state to state. Some people say this is unjust because it is "unequal," so that the federal government should impose one-size-fits-all laws and policies on the states. Although the United States Constitution prohibits the federal government from doing so, it isn't difficult to find workarounds. For example, since the federal government can raise vastly greater amounts of revenue than any state can, Washington can wield a carrot rather than a stick—offering federal funds to cash-starved state governments as a reward for adopting the policies that Big Daddy designs.

The fallacy in the antifederalism argument lies in taking "equal" to mean "identical." By this reasoning, it is also a violation of equality for Johnny's parents to make rules for Johnny but for Ruthie's parents to make rules for Ruthie. Every family should be forced to have the same rules; better yet, all children should be raised by government. But no: Despite their mistakes, on the whole parents will make better decisions for their children than could the state.

What about other definitions of the proper work of government, such as "protecting the rights of the people"? Provided that we take "the people" to include not only individuals, but also their forms of association, such as families and churches, doesn't this come to pretty much the same thing? It does, if we use terms like "rights" in the way our ancestors did, but we don't any more. One of the battlefronts in the culture wars is to capture the prestige of the word "rights" for things that would never have been considered "rights" previously. For example, our ancestors would have affirmed a right to the free exercise of religion. But now, social justice warriors say that since there is a right to be free from discrimination, the religious teaching that marriage is a union of a man and a woman must be suppressed; that since there is a right to equality, religious schools must be forced to accept teachers who deny religious teaching; that since there is a right to abortion, euthanasia, and assisted suicide, doctors and nurses who object to these procedures on grounds of conscience must be compelled to participate in them—and that others who object to them should be compelled to subsidize them, through forced contributions of one sort or another.

What makes such abuses possible is the fact that the idea of human rights has been severed from its foundation in objective natural law, and re-planted in subjective human willfulness. Unfortunately, there is no such thing as a principle which cannot be abused. Not even subsidiarity can be defined so precisely that distortion is impossible. The greatest truths have always been parasitized by the greatest lies. Advocates of injustice always speak of justice; advocates of wrong always prate of right.

This will continue. The only bulwark against it is to be aware of what is happening, and to think as clearly as possible.

Lunacy 9

Scientists, Scholars, and Experts Are Neutral Authorities

❧

Through the aid of applied science we shall rise from partisanship into patriotism.[*]

In 1927, Julian Benda published a book provocatively titled *The Treason of the Intellectuals,* arguing that although in former days, most of the intellectual class stood apart from political passions, today they plunge into them, scorning the attitude of critical suspension from rivalries.

Benda may not have been right that intellectuals were less tainted by political passions formerly than in modern times. Counterexamples abound. Consider Vergil, who wrote the *Aeneid* to justify the Roman empire's glorious destiny to rule forever.

My own argument is more modest. It is possible, however difficult, for an intellectual to be objective. This claim is psychological. It is *impossible*, though, for an intellectual to be neutral. This claim is not psychological, but

---

* David Starr Jordan, *The Call of the Nation* (1910).

logical. The concept of making judgments without any biases or assumptions makes no more sense than the concept of a tightly packed vacuum. Even to side *with* objectivity *against* blind partisanship is already to take a side—and that is only the beginning.

Efforts to find some neutral ground for adjudicating disputes are doomed to failure. For example, many people think that moral disagreements can be settled by the supposedly neutral rule of not harming others. But even in order to follow such a rule, we would have to agree about what counts as harming others. Does only physical harm count as harm? What about emotional harm, such as having one's feelings hurt? What about moral harm, such as corruption, seduction, or convincing someone else of a lie? Should we include only harms which result from doing things, such as assassinating our enemies? Or should we also include harms which result from *not* doing things, such as neglecting our children? Should we include *deserved* harms, like being imprisoned as punishment for crime? What about harms that do us good, such as the tedium of being forced to do arithmetic exercises during school? There is nothing neutral about any of these decisions. Harm is bad—but the reason it is so easy to get people to agree to this proposition is that by leaving what counts as harm unspecified, we sweep the hard questions under the rug.

Similar sleight of hand is involved when we "agree to disagree," honor "choice," or say "let's just be tolerant." Agreeing to disagree with the mugger means that he gets to mug me, but I get to be unhappy about it. I am free to choose not to be robbed, but he is free to choose to rob me. No doubt tolerating what ought to be tolerated is a virtue, but there lies the question, doesn't it? What ought to be? Virtue lies in a mean. Error lies in not only in failing to tolerate what should be, but also in tolerating what shouldn't.

In fact, so-called neutrality is really bad-faith authoritarianism. It is a pulling of wool over the eyes. Whatever view succeeds in passing itself off as neutral wins without having to make a case for itself. *Someone's* opinion of what should be done prevails over *someone else's* opinion about the matter, merely through the pretense that it is not an opinion about what should be done.

These examples concern moral issues, but contrary to supposed "fact checkers," the same point applies to scientific and policy issues. Dr. Anthony Fauci, public face of the White House Coronavirus Task Force during most of the COVID-19 pandemic, complained that his critics were "really criticizing science because I represent science. That's dangerous. To me, that's more dangerous than the slings and the arrows that get thrown at me. I'm not going to be around here forever, but science is going to be here forever. And if you damage science, you are doing something very detrimental to society long after I leave. And that's what I worry about."[1]

The director was claiming that the judgments of the authorities were neutral, and therefore should be accepted, *because they were scientific, not political*. Yes, they really were scientific—but no, that did not make them neutral. Notice that these authorities did not confine themselves to saying that the risk of contracting COVID could be minimized only through radical social distancing measures. Rather they said everyone *should* undertake these measures. In effect, they were making the political judgment that a single factor, the danger of infection, trumped all other factors. Factors like what? Like depression, suicide, and alcohol abuse because of social isolation; like educational deficits among children because schools are closed; like unemployment and economic hardship because businesses and factories are shut down.

Suppose the authorities *had* confined themselves to their role, not saying, "Do this," but only claiming, "By doing this, the single danger of infection would be minimized." Would they then have been neutral? No. Numerous highly credentialed and well-known epidemiologists not part of the government bureaucracy dissented from its conclusions—and their judgments were scientific, too. More than 900,000 health professionals signed what was called the Great Barrington Declaration,[2] which urged a different approach to the control of infection. This alternative approach, which they called "Focused Protection," would have given priority to persons most at risk. Leaked emails showed that rather than engaging honestly with such dissenters, Dr. Fauci took steps to discredit the declaration, calling its originators "fringe" epidemiologists. Yet as Dr. Fauci admitted to the House Select Committee on the

Coronavirus Pandemic on January 8, 2024, the social distancing recommendations he promoted were not based on science but "sort of just appeared."[3]

Suppose the authorities *had* worked out their recommendations through an honest engagement with scientists of other views. *Then* would they have been neutral? No. In that case they would have attained the very great virtue of objectivity, but they still would not have been neutral. It is both possible and desirable to be objective, but it is nonsensical to pretend to neutrality. The mistake lies in confusing neutrality with objectivity. Objectivity is like fairness in sports, which isn't having *no* bias but having a bias in favor of skill over team partisanship. Similarly, objectivity is having a bias for truth over "being right," having a willingness to be proven wrong, and adhering to a set of norms for discussion that maximize the chances of reaching a true consensus while minimizing the risks of reaching a false one.

At every stage, even the most objective procedures require decisions, and any decision for P is a decision against Q. Whoever formulates a scientific hypothesis formulates *some* scientific hypothesis; whoever compares hypotheses compares *certain* hypotheses out of the infinity of possible hypotheses; whoever subjects hypotheses to tests formulates *certain* tests, judging which evidence is most germane and which methods of weighing it most appropriate.

This is why honest scientists sometimes have to swallow their pride, change their minds, and even confess fault. In 2024, a disturbing article by Nicholas Wade detailed the mounting evidence that the COVID virus not only leaked from a lab but was manufactured there. Yet prying this information from the experts was not easy. Wade, a science journalist, was attacked for his arguments. He argued in the *Wall Street Journal* that members of his profession were "too beholden to their sources to suspect that virologists would lie to them about the extent of their profession's responsibility for a catastrophic pandemic."[4]

Expert judgment easily goes wrong even when everyone is honest. At one point in the twentieth century, climatologists were convinced that the world was becoming colder. Geologists considered the idea of continents moving absurd. Still earlier, the evidence for the hypothesis that the sun orbits the earth seemed at least as good as the evidence for the contrary view. Spatial location was thought to be not relative but absolute. Atoms were considered indivisible and impenetrable.

Conclusions about such things have changed, and may change again, in unanticipated ways. Species were once considered the products of divine design; then, after Darwin, they came to be viewed as the results of a meaningless process that did not have them in mind. Now some biologists and biochemists are having second thoughts, because although random mutation plus natural selection seems able to explain some things, such as changes in the sizes of finch beaks, it faces grave difficulties when confronted with other things, such as what biochemist Michael Behe calls "irreducible complexity"—complexity which could not have arisen through a sequence of small changes each of which had adaptive value.[5]

Can we be neutral? No. Can we be objective? Yes, but this is excruciatingly difficult.

One difficulty is that the urge to greater certainty than we can attain tempts us to rush, blurring very different questions. For example, it is one thing to ask whether the earth is warming, but another to ask how sure we can be and how we might be wrong. It is one thing to ask whether warming is real, but another to ask whether it has been caused by human activity. It is one thing to ask whether we can do anything about it, but another to ask whether we *should* do anything about it. It is one thing to ask what good we might do by trying, and another to ask how we might do harm. For that matter, it is one thing to ask what bad effects warming itself might have, and another to ask about possible good ones. The answer to one question does not imply the answer to another.

Another risk is panicking. The danger of *mistaken* conclusions about global warming might be great; there are risks both in underestimating and overestimating climate change. But it is easier to capture the public imagination by conjuring up extreme scenarios of the earth turning into a desert. Panic may also lead us to trust dubious data and make us feel justified in suppressing dissent. In the "Climategate" scandal at the Climatic Research Unit of the University of East Anglia, England, leaked email messages gave strong reason to believe that researchers had colluded to manipulate data, interfere with the peer-review process, and punish scientists who dissented from their conclusions. Though official investigators drew milder conclusions, even they criticized the university for a "culture of withholding information."

We may *prefer* certain answers, whether they are justified or not. Those who favor small government might minimize global warming risk, discourage big policy changes, and emphasize the adaptability of markets to new conditions. But those who favor big government may be inclined to maximize the risk, propose radical changes, and overrule markets. Who stands to gain or lose may also make a difference. No one would be surprised if selenium miners emphasized the threat of global warming more than coal miners, since selenium is used in solar cells.

Researchers who suggest extreme scenarios may also find it easier to be published or to obtain research grants. The bias of professional journals in favor of positive results is well known. "We found P to affect Q"—accept. "We found no effect"—reject.[6] John Ioannis and others have found that, largely for such reasons, most published findings in medical research are false.[7]

Finally, intellectuals are no less inclined to groupthink than anyone else. Humans are social creatures. Our willingness to cooperate makes science and scholarship possible, but our desire for the approval of our peers makes us reluctant to buck the crowd. It is not entirely possible to be immune from peer pressure, but we can try to find more appropriate peers, always remaining open to outside criticism.

The modern age is sometimes thought to be the age of the common man, but this is a myth; it is the age of the expert. Experts, unfortunately, make better servants than they do rulers, for the best rulers are not experts but wise men. Of course, wise men should not be trusted to nominate themselves any more than experts should be. Even in this age of mass delusions, ordinary people are usually better able to recognize who is truly wise and who is not. However indispensable expert knowledge may be, in the end the expert's conclusion is as much a *judgment* as is the opinion of the fellow on the next barstool.

Lunacy 10

Democracy Is the Literal Rule of the People

∾

In framing a government which is to be administered by men over men, the great difficulty lies in this: you must first enable the government to control the governed; and in the next place oblige it to control itself. A dependence on the people is, no doubt, the primary control on the government; but experience has taught mankind the necessity of auxiliary precautions.[*]

A television pundit said recently, "There is a movement to take power from the party elites and return it to the people." Nonsense. But as I have been saying, even nonsense must contain some truth, or else no one could swallow it.

We do see a rising suspicion of our elites—not just party bosses, but union bosses, corporate bosses, judges, bureaucrats, and experts of various kinds. This suspicion is well deserved. Two recent studies by the Rasmussen polling organization, RMG Research, delved into the views of elites, defining them as people with at least one postgraduate degree, earning more than $150,000, and living in ZIP codes where the population density exceeds 10,000 per square mile. It isn't surprising that the opinions of elites differed strongly

---

[*] *Federalist*, no. 51 (1788).

from those of ordinary people over a wide range of topics. However, the questions covered more than political party preferences, tax rates, and current affairs. Respondents were also asked whether they would rather cheat than lose a close election. Seven percent of all voters said yes; 35 percent of elite voters said yes; and among those elite voters who talked about politics every day, 69 percent said yes. Anyone who doesn't find this result disturbing has a moral screw loose.[1]

But let us think clearly: In no conceivable world could we *all rule at once over all of us at once.* The rulers and ruled are always different people. Even in what we call self-government, some rule, others don't.

In fact, there is a ruling element in every organized whole. We say that people of good moral character can rule themselves, but that those of weak character can't. This is true, but as stated, it is misleading. Command implies that there is a difference between the element that commands and the element that follows. A single person cannot command and follow in the same sense, any more than he can lift himself into the air by raising his hands, taking a grip on his shoulders, and pulling up. What we really mean by self-rule is that reason, the noblest element in us, rules our other elements, such as our passions and appetites.

If there are always some who rule and others who don't, that doesn't mean that there is no such thing as a republic. The questions are *who* rules, *how they get* to rule, and *how* they rule. In a well-ordered republic, the ruled have at least some choice in the matter. Moreover—and this is even more important—ideally they choose the best among them to rule, those who express the best within them. So that the situation doesn't degenerate, this arrangement also requires that the rulers be subject to certain limits, and that they put themselves under the same rules they make for others. There are a few more pragmatic requirements, too, such as rotation in office.

The closest things to literal "rule by the people" would be ancient Greek democracies and old New England town meetings, in which all decisions were made in assemblies which citizens could attend personally. To say "closest," though, is not to say "close." A rubber balloon may be the closest children's toy to a jellyfish, but it is not very like a jellyfish. Even in the ancient popular assemblies, some citizens had influence, others didn't; some were heard respectfully, some weren't; and some were shouted down. Anyone who has ever participated in a committee meeting with what are called "strong personalities" knows how that can work.

Moreover, when popular assemblies grow large, they also grow riotous and chaotic, which is why the founders of the American republic had so little respect for them. Try to imagine a popular assembly of several hundred million adult citizens. Could they have a real discussion? Would all voices be heard and considered? Would there even be time? They might all be electronically polled, but an opinion poll is hardly a deliberative conversation, and cannot be made to resemble one except by trickery and stagecraft. Some voices would inevitably dominate. Consider what happens in our social media.

Although our own country is much too large for popular assemblies, we flatter ourselves that in our sort of republic the people rule through the delegates whom they choose. But even if these delegates made all the decisions—which is certainly not the case, for in most matters, our legislators pass the buck to an elephantine regulatory bureaucracy—this would still not be rule by the people. At most it would be rule by the chosen delegates of the people. The Greek thinkers would have considered "representative democracy" a contradiction in terms. They considered rule by delegates not a form of democracy, but a form of oligarchy, and with good reason. Some people have more influence over who is selected to rule, some less. People of some kinds and classes are more likely to be selected, some less.

In fact, depending on *which* kinds of people are more likely to be selected, this may be a good thing. We should *prefer* some kinds of people to be selected.

So which kinds? The most famous in show business? Not a good idea, although it is not impossible for an entertainer to be qualified. The most opulently wealthy? Hardly, although if they have attained their wealth through useful enterprise, they have some claim to consideration. The most highly educated? A broadly liberal education and a large fund of knowledge are good things, but intellectuals make better servants than rulers. The historian Paul Johnson—obviously an intellectual himself, as am I—points out that

> intellectuals, far from being highly individualistic and non-conformist people, follow certain regular patterns of behavior. Taken as a group, they are often ultra-conformist within the circles formed by those whose approval they seek and value. That is what makes them, *en masse*, so dangerous, for it enables them to create climates of opinion and prevailing orthodoxies, which themselves often generate irrational and destructive courses of action.

He concludes, "The worst of all despotisms is the heartless tyranny of ideas."[2]

Who, then? The most mediocre? Senator Roman Hruska once remarked about Judge G. Harrold Carswell, who had been nominated for the U.S. Supreme Court by President Richard Nixon but was considered a lightweight, "Even if he were mediocre, there are a lot of mediocre judges and people and lawyers. They are entitled to a little representation, aren't they, and a little chance?"[3] Not in that sense. We should certainly demand that those who rule respect the interests and concerns of people who are middling in judgment and virtue—but we should prefer *to be ruled* by those who are greatest in judgment and virtue. To the extent that a republic tends to bring this about, it is a good thing. When it no longer can, it may not be.

In fact, the best argument for mediocrity is not that it is mediocre, but that it may protect us from those with the *least* judgment and moral character. As William F. Buckley Jr. once wrote, "I should sooner live in a society governed by the first two thousand names in the Boston telephone directory than in a society governed by the two thousand faculty members of Harvard University." He wasn't endorsing mediocrity *as such*, for he went on to say, "Not, heaven knows, because I hold lightly the brainpower or knowledge or generosity or even the affability of the Harvard faculty: but because I greatly fear intellectual arrogance, and that is a distinguishing characteristic of the university which refuses to accept any common premise."[4]

The composition of every elite changes over time, and most elites are mixtures of various groups. During any given era the members of the elite may be mostly aristocrats, entrepreneurs, executives of old and established businesses, professionals, labor bosses, guild masters, priests, machine politicians, or who knows what. Some make decisions, some influence them; others broker deals.

In our own regime, the most important rules are made not by lawmakers, but by administrators and judges, and we have far less choice over who enters those two groups. So much depends on the gatekeepers. The professions largely govern themselves, which is good if their members are modest, prudent, and virtuous, but not if they are arrogant, reckless, and depraved. Even the arrogant and reckless will probably *believe* themselves virtuous, even if according to a depraved understanding of virtue. As our ancestors said, no man can judge his own case.

How elites work is often different from how it seems, and I don't necessarily mean because of crookedness, deception, or conspiracies. For example, it is simply untrue that big business today exerts influence in favor of capitalism. If capitalism means free markets, it has been quite a long time since capitalists believed in capitalism, which is why Wall Street is now more generally allied with the political Left. One might argue that capitalists *never did* believe in capitalism, for the anticapitalist motives of capitalists have been recognized since Adam Smith. That's why he railed against privileges and monopolies. The free-market revolution was not so much about the rise of a business class as it was the rise of a belief *among* this rising class, a belief that competition, rather than favoritism, was the best way to get ahead. That belief is dying, because the dominant psychological and organizational type of capitalist is no longer the entrepreneur, but the bureaucrat. Economies and technologies of scale require large organizations; large organizations dislike rivals; and second-generation managers don't burn with the founder's own fire. Nowadays even real entrepreneurs try to convert themselves into government dependents as quickly as they can. Tesla and SpaceX would be nothing without governmental patronage. This is less like free enterprise than like socialism with outsourcing.

If choosing our elites means simply putting them in power, we can't usually choose our elites. However, we *can* sometimes tweak things. For example, we can tweak our universities so that new elements enter by merit, rather than by the old-boy system or by group politics. We can also tweak the constitutional advantages of different groups so that they are forced to deal with each other. Long ago in England, the decision was made that the knights, who were the lowest rank of gentlemen, would sit in the House of Commons with influential plain folk, rather than in the House of Lords with the barons. This placed the nobility and the commoners more nearly on a level. Since it was in the self-interest of the Crown, as balancer, not to let *either* group dominate, this arrangement was made so that neither side of the great divide could easily do injustice to the other. At least that was the hope.

Our kind of republic was a novel invention. Unfortunately, new technologies for making elites irresponsible to those whom they supposedly serve have distorted it. To mention but a few: the development of addictive social media; the spread of mood management drugs, not just to treat clinical depression but to make unhappy people think everything is fine; the political organization of deviance; the whetting of tribal hatreds; the cultivation of permanent crisis; the development of universal omniscient surveillance; the harvesting of vast amounts of personal information about everyday individuals from their apps and electronic devices; the blending of the methods of political organization with those of protection rackets; the making of so many laws that no one can be sure he is in compliance; the handoff of rule-making power from legislatures to administrative agencies; the promotion of the idea of a "living" constitution so that law comes to mean whatever those in power say it means; and the domestic use of techniques which were first developed for psychological warfare against enemies.

In short, not even a republic is the literal "rule of the people." But a system in which elites are responsible to those they govern is a possible, though delicate, achievement.

III

Delusions About Family and Sexuality

Almost all the miseries of life, almost all the wickedness that infects society, and almost all the distresses that afflict mankind, are the consequences of some defect in private duties. Likewise, all the joys of this world may be attributable to the happiness of hearth and home.

—Samuel Johnson, *Gleanings from Johnson*

Lunacy 11

Uncoupling Sex from Its
Consequences Has No Consequences

❧

It feels like we were tricked into exploiting ourselves [and] tricked into thinking it was our idea.[*]

Sex has natural consequences. Some of them may not be desired, and the most widespread view of sexual ethics today is based on avoiding them. Can intercourse spread disease? Then wash often, change the sheets, and use condoms. Can it cause pregnancy? Then use contraceptives and hold abortion in reserve. In the old days, the argument runs, we couldn't uncouple sex from its consequences, so virtue meant chastity. Today we can, so virtue means "safe sex."

The older view of the sexual powers didn't neglect their natural consequences; it focused instead on their natural purposes. Just how thoroughly this older view has been forgotten has been brought home to me through

---

[*] "Katie," quoted in Madeleine Holden, "These Gen Z Women Think Sex Positivity Is Overrated," *Buzzfeed* (July 29, 2021), https://www.buzzfeednews.com/article/madeleineholden/gen-z-sex-positivity/.

teaching. If I ask my students, "What is the natural purpose of the sexual powers?" they inevitably reply, "Pleasure." But there is something wrong with this answer. The exercise of every voluntary power is pleasurable, yet its purpose always lies elsewhere. For instance, the pleasure of eating may give me a motive to eat, but the natural purpose of eating isn't pleasure, but maintaining my body. In fact, if I treat pleasure itself as its purpose, I will eat whenever it is pleasurable, even to the destruction of my health. So these days, I begin by asking not about the natural purposes of the sexual powers, but about the natural purposes of other things, like eating. *Then* when I ask about the natural purposes of the sexual powers, my students reply, "Procreation," perhaps adding, "Bonding the mother and father."

These days, even the rare proponents of abstinence tend to base their arguments on natural consequences rather than natural purposes, pointing out that so-called safe sex isn't completely safe. One can still be infected. One can still conceive. To most people such arguments seem pretty weak. Even a careful driver may have an accident, but we don't stop driving on roads.

What both sides overlook is that the very attempt to uncouple sex from its natural consequences has consequences. Let's call overlooking this fact the uncoupling delusion, and those who hold it uncouplers.

It was once believed among uncouplers that the advent of modern contraceptives would do away with unwed pregnancies. What has actually happened is that despite the use of the Pill, the rate of unwed pregnancies has skyrocketed. In 1940, 4 percent of U.S. children were born to single mothers. By 2021, the rate had increased tenfold, to 40 percent.[1] Yes, one person, using contraceptives, is less likely to conceive. But in the aggregate, the advent of contraceptives has so radically changed *attitudes* toward sex—"It's okay now!"—that far more people are having casual intercourse *with or without* contraceptives.

Uncouplers will be similarly disappointed if they expect antibacterials and antivirals to eliminate the threat of sexually transmitted diseases. Certainly such medicines help at the individual level, but again, in the aggregate, overconfidence in them encourages such great changes in behavior that these diseases actually have become more prevalent rather than less. In the scant five years between 2016 and 2020, the overall rate of venereal disease increased 11 percent. This figure includes gonorrhea, which climbed 45 percent; total syphilis, which climbed 52 percent; and syphilis among newborns, which exploded by a staggering 235 percent.[2] These are *curable* infections. Let us remember that other STDs, such as hepatitis B, herpes simplex, HIV, and human papilloma virus, are incurable.

To uncouplers, the solution to these unintended consequences of our attempts to eliminate consequences seems obvious. We must educate about safe sex even more aggressively, especially among young people, and distribute free condoms to high school students. Insanity has been famously defined as doing the same thing repeatedly and expecting a different result. Here is insanity.

Consider too *why* people are so reluctant to use condoms and other methods of "safe sex."

Researcher Patricia Stearn reports that the most common reason inner-city white teens in steady relationships give for not using condoms is that "unprotected sex is a pledge of intimacy and trust which elevates 'f-----' to 'making love.'"[3] In fact, this attitude is current far beyond the inner city, and sex educators devote a great deal of futile energy to undermining it. Yet here again they are going against one of the natural consequences of sex: It *bonds us, we want it* to bond us, and at some level *we want it to be fruitful.* Condoms are often called "barrier methods" of contraception. The term is unintentionally revealing, because they place a wall between the bodies of two persons whose very act means, "Let us become one!"

But uncouplers would like to separate sex from that sort of natural consequence, too. Why *should* we allow ourselves to feel bonded? It's *not* natural, they say. It's just a bad habit, a vestige of an obsolete moral scruple. Instead of making love, just hook up: no commitment, no connection, no personal communion.

Know what? It doesn't work. We aren't designed for that. Often the parties who hook up have to get drunk just to go through with it. Often they feel empty afterward. Women, especially, report feeling depressed after breaking up with a "f--- buddy," even though supposedly there is nothing to "break" because they haven't any bond. Men who have sex with one woman after another report that they lose any ability for real intimacy. Since at some level they know they have treated their girlfriends like dirt, they also suffer a diminished sense of manhood and a reluctance to grow up.

But if we are going to separate sex from the natural consequence of bonding and desiring to bond, why bother with other persons at all? Why not just use porn? As it turns out, pornography use, too, has natural consequences. One should have expected this, because a real love partner, another person, is endlessly fascinating, while mere images "get old." The sort of pornography which once stimulated loses its power to excite, and one begins to seek a greater jolt. Once this cycle begins, there is no easy way to end it. Mary Harrington reports, "In a 2021 survey of approximately 5,000 American college students, 58 percent of women reported having been choked during sex. This is often non-consensual and inspired by porn. A survey commissioned by the BBC in 2020 found that 71 percent of British men under 40 have slapped, choked, or spat on a partner during sex, with more than half stating that porn had influenced their desire to do so."[4]

I suspect that most of these spitters, slappers, and chokers would agree that, in sex, anything goes "so long as it doesn't hurt anyone"—that's what we say now, isn't it?—but the definition of hurt seems elastic. How do uncouplers respond to such problems? Simple: by rebranding them as solutions. Nona Willis Aronowitz writes in the *New York Times,* "I do believe that reaching for more sexual freedom, not less—the freedom to have whatever kind of sex we want, including, yes, casual sex and choking sex and porny sex—is still the only way we can hope to solve the problems of our current sexual landscape."[5] If choking sex is not a "problem," one wonders what is.

Prodigious levels of blindness and self-deception are necessary to support this line of thinking. Consider a *New York Times* opinion piece by Anna Louie Sussman. She admits that the overwhelming evidence that women and their children do better when they are married to the fathers "may well be true." Yet she complains that those who urge women to seek marriage are "scolds" who are "harping from on high." Why? Because men are of such low quality today that few would make good marriage partners. It never occurs to her to ask why a man who isn't good enough to marry is good enough to sleep with and have babies with.[6]

We are beginning to see signs of pushback, especially among women. Speaking for those now raising children, Jennifer Moses comments that her generation was "the first not only to be free of old-fashioned fears about our reputations but actually pressured by our peers and the wider culture to find our true womanhood in the bedroom." In her circle of grown-up girlfriends, "I don't know one of them who doesn't have feelings of lingering discomfort regarding her own sexual past. And not one woman I've ever asked about the subject has said that she wishes she'd 'experimented' more."[7]

Pressure on young women to have casual sex continues to come not only from young men but also from their peers. Yet younger women are beginning to push back too. Meghan Dillon writes in *Evie* magazine:

> I was hanging out with a group of girlfriends one night at college when one suggested I should have sex with one of my guy friends. . . . This wasn't them trying to help me out. This felt like a scene from *Mean Girls*. Some suggested that no guy would want to date me because of my virginity . . . and that I should just "get it over with." . . . I told them that sex was a big deal to me, and I didn't want to give it up for a one-night stand and ruin a friendship. But they refused to back down, so I left with another friend when I couldn't take it anymore.[8]

In the final analysis we must decide whether we really *want* sex to be beautiful; I hope we do. We must also refuse to yield to the temptation to despair. One day I remarked to my students that although my generation had invented the sexual revolution, I thought theirs was paying the price. A young man remarked that he knew what I meant. More than anything, he said, he wanted to fall in love with a woman, marry her, and be faithful to her forever. Tragically, he added, "But I don't think it's possible." He did want beauty, but was unwilling to think he could do better than his parents, who had botched their own love badly.

That kind of hope need not die. We can invite forfeited beauty to return.

Lunacy 12

Both Sexes Must Make the Same Choices

∞

*No, we don't believe that any woman should have this choice. No woman should
be authorized to stay at home to raise her children. Society should be totally
different. Women should not have that choice, precisely because if there is such
a choice, too many women will make that one. It is a way of forcing women in a
certain direction.*[*]

In *My Fair Lady,* the notorious Professor Higgins asks, "Why can't a woman be more like a man?"

Why does every one do what the others do?
Can't a woman learn to use her head?
Why do they do everything their mothers do?
Why don't they grow up—well, like their father instead?[1]

We associate this idea with men, but the anthem is sung by women too—especially by those competing in historically male fields. Consider the remarks of Shulamit Kahn, a professor of economics at Boston University. Professor Kahn coauthored a study which found that in science, women do

---

just as well as men in applying for grants, submitting journal articles, and asking for recommendation letters, and actually do better than men in applying for tenure-track jobs. However, when the *Wall Street Journal* lauded her findings in an editorial titled "Women in Science Are Doing All Right,"[2] she blasted back that women in science are *not* doing all right:

> [W]omen, especially in life sciences, aren't applying to tenure-track jobs in the first place in proportions commensurate with their number of newly minted PhDs. Some may conclude, "That's their choice." But the literature says that the major reason women PhDs don't apply to tenure-track jobs is that they look ahead to the four or five years of postdocs required in many fields and the six-year deadline to amass a tenure dossier, compare it to their biological clocks ticking away, and instead choose industry, government or nontenure-track academic jobs. That is not "all right" if we want our best and brightest, men or women, to be the ones running university research labs and educating the next generation of PhDs.[3]

Women, you have been warned. It's not all right for you to heed your biological clock. It's entirely wrong for you to prefer a career that doesn't foreclose the possibility of having children. Bright scientists are ever so much better than bright mothers. Technically training the next generation is ever so much more important than bringing it into being.

Professor Kahn agrees with Professor Higgins: Why can't women be more like men? Men don't worry about their biological clocks. Why shouldn't women pretend that they don't need to either?

One would have thought that being pro-woman would mean being pro-womanhood. Apparently not.

The attitude that equality requires both sexes to make the same choices is prevalent in other areas too. Consider sex. The old double standard, winking at unchaste men while shaming unchaste women, was loathsome. Sheer honesty, however, demands recognition that women are by nature more cautious and protective of their bodies. The advent of contraceptives gave promiscuous men an excuse to demand that women suppress their natural modesty and be ready to "put out" at any time. Yes, the double standard has been abolished—but to the disadvantage of women. In the resulting porno-topia, the sexual expectations of males become cruel. Teen girls are rewarded with social media "likes" for taking off their clothes—"the more skin, the more likes." Men are conditioned to find female characters in action films "hot" for committing or suffering violence.

Although the equal dignity of men and women requires respect for their differences, increasingly we demand that differences be ignored or abolished. After COVID, economists complained that women took longer than men to return to the workplace. Health officials have considered whether women in the military should be drugged to suppress their natural monthly periods. Since men can't be mothers, equality with men is deemed to require the ability to make motherhood unhappen. Giving women greater protection from industrial chemicals than men because of their greater vulnerability is considered discriminatory.

Insisting that the sexes be the same works against males too. Boys are drugged not just for genuine attention disorders, but because they are wigglier and have more difficulty sitting still in the classroom. They have fallen behind not only in the lower grades but in college, where girls are a strong majority. This depresses male earning ability, so that young women, who tend to marry up, find them less appropriate mates.

Sociologist Rosemary Hopcroft remarks, "There is a difference between eliminating barriers to female participation in the workforce and incentivizing equal employment outcomes for men and women. While laws and policies that limit opportunities for women are unwarranted, stipulating that all workplaces must have the same proportion of men and women, or incentivizing or otherwise encouraging men and women to act in exactly the same way, will likely have negative consequences." She reasons that "because of sex differences regarding parenting in particular, these policies are likely to inhibit family formation and childbearing. For example, to the extent that such laws or policies mean that women replace men in well-paid jobs, one effect will be that more men end up in jobs that cannot support a family." Among other things, "This means less childbearing among poorer couples."[4]

What *are* the sexes anyway? When nominee Ketanji Brown Jackson refused during her U.S. Supreme Court confirmation hearings to define "woman," replying, "I'm not a biologist," *USA Today* smugly commented, "A competent biologist would not be able to offer a definitive answer either."[5]

Oh? A woman is a human being of the sex whose members are potentially mothers, and a man is a human being of the sex whose members are potentially fathers. This is not mysterious. No competent biologist should be befuddled about the distinction. All other sexual differences derive from it.[6]

Potentiality is not the same as physical possibility. Although an infertile woman is unable to conceive, she suffers not the lack of potentiality for motherhood, but a block to its physical expression. Moreover, having children is not the only expression of the potentialities for motherhood and fatherhood. A man who fails to care for his children and their mother has failed as a father. And as Alice von Hildebrand remarks, even a woman who is not a physical mother may be a psychological or spiritual mother.[7]

A man cannot speak from inside the experience of womanhood. Yet even from the outside it plainly differs profoundly from manhood. I love my children deeply, but I didn't carry them inside my body or nourish them from my breasts. My wife, who did, is connected with them in an intimate, physical bond which men cannot experience, and which conditioned her feelings toward them, toward herself, and toward everyone else. These differences also illuminate other differences for which each sex is sometimes wrongly criticized. Women, who carry in themselves the future of the human race, *need* to be more protective of their bodies, and men, to keep them safe, need to be less. As their courage takes different forms, so does their love. Both can nurture their children, but she will be more resolute that even discipline requires tenderness, and he, that even tenderness requires discipline.

Potentiality for motherhood knits together a woman's qualities and makes sense of her difference from his. Edith Stein reminds us that men are more prone to abstractions, while women tend to focus on the concrete. Men don't mind impersonality, but women are more attuned to relational nuance. Men tend to be specialists and single-taskers, developing certain talents to do things in the world. Women tend to be generalists and multitaskers, cultivating a well-rounded development of their abilities and using them to nurture the life around them.[8] These broad differences are only to be expected in view of the fundamental sexual difference in potentiality for fatherhood or motherhood. Consider that multitasking talent. In view of what it takes to run a home, doesn't it make sense for women, on average, to have more of it? A mother must be a center of peace for her family—even though the soup is ready, Susie needs to nurse, Billy skinned his knee, and the telephone, timer, and doorbell are ringing all at once.

Though men incline more to tending their careers, and women their families, of course not all women will, or must, pursue an exclusively domestic life. Even so, the potentiality for motherhood changes everything. Women who pursue a career and have free choice tend to choose careers that allow them to give first place to caring for their children. They typically prefer pursuits that give greater scope to maternal qualities, and even when a woman chooses a traditionally masculine career, she tends to perform it in ways that allow her to exercise her maternal qualities. A male attorney will probably focus intensely on the properties of the task itself. This worthy trait makes it easy for him to lose sight of the humanity of his clients. Can he *learn* to remember their humanity? Yes, but he is much more likely to need the reminder in the first place. A female attorney may find the abstract quality of the law somewhat alienating, even while admitting its necessity. On the other hand, she is much less likely to forget that she is dealing with human beings.

It is no cliché that manhood is outward directed, womanhood inward directed. Outward-directedness is not the same as *other*-directedness, for many men prefer dealing with things. Inward-directedness is not the same as *self*-directedness, for the feminine genius includes caring for her local circle. It is a good thing that an unmarried man pursues the beloved, whereas an unmarried woman makes herself attractive to pursuit; it is a good thing that a husband protects the home, whereas a wife establishes it on the hearth; it is a good thing that a father represents and oversees the family, whereas a mother conducts and manages it.

Today it has become almost embarrassing to read things like these. Contrasts between fathers and mothers seem naïve, nostalgic, sentimental, stereotypical, offensive, even embarrassing. We have turned husbands and wives into "spouses," fathers and mothers into "parent figures." Moreover, most of us have a dimmer conception of fatherhood than of motherhood. One reason may be that a father's connection with his children is not mediated by his body in the way a mother's is. A darker one is that paternal absenteeism and other forms of masculine failure are so conspicuous today. Open mockery of fathers, a fixture of popular culture, is surely both a cause and an effect.

Once upon a time the differences between men and women were not thought so strange, unmentionable, and confusing. We have a long quest and a difficult journey to make before we can speak of them again with ease and gaiety.

Lunacy 13

Marriage Can Be Whatever We Want It to Be

∽

[W]e must be creative in the ways we use [sexual] force to evolve new and appro-priate ways to solve our problems and to make each other and ourselves happy.[*]

Matrimony is a natural institution. Its natural purpose is to give children a fighting chance of being raised by their mothers and fathers. Other species procreate differently. Guppies cooperate only for a moment, don't know their children, and may even eat them. We love our children, and the distinctly human mode of procreation is profoundly personal, featuring an enduring partnership between the man and the woman, who are different in ways that enable them to balance and complement each other.[1]

In making the child, the female provides the egg, the male fertilizes it, and the female incubates the zygote. In raising the child, the male is more suited to protect, the female to nurture. In teaching the child, male and female

---

*   Morning Glory Zell, "A Bouquet of Lovers," *Green Egg* 23 no. 89 (May 1990), https://web.archive.org/web/20030508180124/http://www.lair.org/writings/polyamory/bouquet.html. The author was the first to give polyamory a name.

provide him with a model of each sex and a model of their relationship. There is no substitute for a mom and dad, and their procreative partnership continues even after the kids are grown, because the kids need the help and counsel of their mothers and fathers to establish their own new families. We are not monads; we are not even merely dyads. We are networks that grow up from dyads.

Children long for their mothers and fathers. The devastation wrought on children by divorce and family breakup is far greater than imagined in the salad days of the early sexual revolution. Family members separated by catastrophes go to heroic lengths to find each other. Though some details of marriage vary according to custom, it does not follow that marriage itself is merely customary, for some arrangements further its natural purpose and others hinder it.

If matrimony were destroyed, it would have to be reinvented. Sociologists Sara McLanahan and Gary Sandefur remark, "If we were asked to design a system for making sure that children's basic needs were met, we would probably come up with something quite similar to the two-parent ideal."[2] The union of man and woman is at the center of our procreative design. Hillary Clinton suggested that "it takes a village to raise a child," but this blurs a crucial distinction. It takes parents to raise children; the village supports the parents.

Since the great majority of human societies have been polygamous, one might be skeptical about claims on behalf of monogamy. Despite the sexual revolution, however, monogamy is spreading around the world, and its advantages have become much more widely recognized. Some have been known for centuries. For example:

1. By eliminating the division of the husband's interest among several wives, monogamy promotes the loving union of wife and husband.
2. By eliminating the division of the father's interest among the children of his various wives, it intensifies their bond with him.
3. By reducing competition among these children, it intensifies their bond with each other.
4. By making men and women more equal, it discourages the develop-

ment of authoritarian personality traits among men, and of servile ones among women. And

5. By diminishing the conflict between rich men who can attract many wives, and poor ones who may not be able to win any, it encourages respect between economic classes and belief in a common good.

Such considerations drove classical natural law thinkers to argue that monogamy best promotes the procreative and unitive goods of sexuality. Though not destroying these goods, polygamy weakens them, and casual sex, obviously, undermines them completely.

Recent work by sociologists Joseph Henrich, Robert Boyd, and Peter J. Richerson amplifies these arguments. To continue my own numbering, they suggest that

6. By limiting sexual competition among men and reducing the numbers of unmarried men, monogamy reduces both crime and personal abuse.

7. By diverting male energy from collecting wives, it increases family savings and time spent by fathers with children.

8. By increasing household relatedness and reducing household conflict, it leads to lower rates of child neglect, abuse, accidental death, and homicide.

9. By reducing competition for younger brides, it narrows the age gap between husband and wife, thereby promoting their equality.

10. By dissipating the pool of unmarried males, it reduces the ability of tyrants to find soldiers and henchmen. And

11. By reducing crime, it weakens tyrants' claims to be the only barrier between citizens and chaos.

Interestingly, the fourth, fifth, tenth, and eleventh of these tendencies would seem to facilitate republican government and undermine despotism. The three authors cautiously agree: "The spread of normative monogamy, which represents a form of egalitarianism, may have helped create the conditions for the emergence of . . . political equality at all levels of government." They point out that the historical record supports this speculation.[3]

One of the most common forms of marital disorder is the rebranding of antimarital arrangements as "alternative" marriages. Often, these so-called alternatives are defended in the name of freedom of choice, but this misses the point dramatically, because the marital relationship is not about the sexual choices of grown-ups, but the well-being of children. Another reason for confusion about them is the idea of the "marriage contract." Don't we arrange the terms of contracts to suit ourselves? Then why can't the marriage contract be whatever we want?

What this thinking overlooks is the very old distinction between *matrimony*, which is the relationship in which husband and wife stand with respect to each other, and *marriage*, which is the act of entering into that relationship. Matrimony—being married—is a status relationship, like being a mother or father, not a contractual relationship, like being a buyer or seller. Marriage—entrance into matrimony—is a contract, yes, in the sense that it requires consent. But the consent of the parties determines only *whether* they are married, not *what* being married is. They are entering a natural institution, the responsibilities and contours of which do not depend on their whims. If they enter something which does depend on their whims, it isn't marriage.

The most radical of supposed alternatives to marriage are "polyamory," "same-sex marriage," and "childfree marriage." It should be obvious that even if polyamory is heterosexual, arbitrary constellations of any number of sexual partners in any combination cannot provide a sound and stable setting for raising children. The dreadful experience of children in the hippie communes of the Sixties should have taught us that, but memories are short. Since "childfree" pairings and same-sex pairings are intrinsically sterile, they have even less to do with marriage. The issue in marriage is not "love," but procreation—more precisely, the issue is the love which hopes to procreate. We link sex with matrimony for a reason: the good of children.

Yet even many who reject the foregoing ideas are often friendly to the ideas of "open marriage," impermanent "marriage," and cohabitation as a sort of practice for marriage.

A majority (51 percent) of adults aged eighteen to twenty-nine say that "open marriages" are acceptable.[4] One woman in such a relationship comments to an interviewer that the problem with monogamy is that it "changes who you are in your marriage, and so long-term, that can be really damaging."[5] Her complaint, apparently, is that commitment changes us. *Yes, and that is the point.* The responsibilities of marriage and children shatter our narrowness and egotism. A man and woman who marry at twenty can expect to be very different persons at twenty-five, and will have changed hand-in-hand. That is the joy of it. Praise God for sleep deprivation and all the other challenges associated with marriage and parenthood that smash our smugness and selfishness. Children are not a lifestyle enhancement. They are themselves.

As to deliberate impermanence: Everyone knows matrimonial union requires work and faces difficulties. But the advent of easy divorce, which was supposed to make things better, has made things worse. It has greatly weakened the motivation to save a troubled marriage; indeed, most divorces now occur in low-conflict marriages. On average, moreover, divorce significantly reduces the well-being of both the spouses and their children.[6] In the decade in which my wife and I wed, instead of vowing "until we are parted by death," some couples intoned the words "so long as it shall be cool for us both." That is not marriage at all. Trust me: It gets easier. Only hang on, and the day may come when you wonder why you ever considered an end to your union.

Finally, as to the so-called committed relationship. The idea that cohabitation is good preparation for marriage is amazingly persistent, considering that it isn't even close to being true. W. Bradford Wilcox has shown that cohabitation is even worse for children than divorce.[7] Research consistently shows that couples who cohabit have poorer relationships *before* marriage, poorer marriages if they *do* marry, and much higher divorce rates *after* marrying. The evidence is so strong that among family sociologists the debate isn't about *whether* couples who cohabit first have weaker marriages, but *why*. One of the most interesting recent findings is that although, in general, women who marry before age thirty or so have a *higher* divorce rate, women who marry in their twenties without having cohabited have some of the *lowest* divorce rates.[8]

The most intuitive explanation is that in every way, the two relationships—matrimony and cohabitation—are fundamentally different. The whole point of matrimony is to cement and formalize a commitment, but the whole point of not being married is to avoid commitment. How can not being committed to someone else be practice for being committed to that person? We would do better to call cohabitation practice for divorce.[9] Besides, matrimony has institutionalized norms. Cohabitation doesn't. You make it up as you go along.

Sociologists suggest additional possibilities. Because a relationship's future is more uncertain in cohabitation, couples have less incentive to invest in it, which makes the future still more uncertain. Just because of this uncertainty, persons who are cohabiting tend to keep score. We do that with merchants: Did I get enough value for what I gave? It shouldn't be necessary with the beloved, but once the habit is formed, it persists into marriage. Besides, couples who don't cohabit have to make a clear decision to enter into the commitment of marriage, but cohabiting couples slide from one stage to another with very little conscious decision.

Here is another explanation. (You may not like it.)

Across human cultures, men tend to prefer the best-looking women. Women care less about men's looks, but prefer men with higher status and greater financial security. As men age, their status and security improve. As women age, their looks decline. Consequently, every year a cohabiting relationship continues, she becomes less attractive to him, but he becomes more attractive to other women. These facts are especially cruel to the woman, who is probably hoping that if only she lives with the man long enough, he will marry her. Actually, the longer the two of them cohabit, the more she is placed at disadvantage—and the more likely he is to want out.

Although cads who ditch their wives for younger women are sometimes envied, they are never admired. However, cohabiting men who walk out on their partners are rarely looked down upon. Furthermore, matrimony civilizes men in a way that cohabitation doesn't. The longer men are married, the more they grow to understand Browning's lines: "Grow old along with me! / The best is yet to be, / The last of life, for which the first was made."

And their wives do look beautiful to them.

Now tell me: How is a relationship which is based on having no commitment, contains multiple incentives for failure, and contains a built-in disadvantage for women, good preparation for getting married? And how is it good for women, for children, for society?

Lunacy 14

Manhood and Womanhood
Can Take Any Shapes That We Wish

∾

Mars-Venus sex differences appear to be as mythical as the Man in the Moon.[*]

If a man is a human being of the sex which possesses the potentiality of fatherhood, and a woman is a human being of the sex which possesses the potentiality of motherhood, it follows that masculinity and femininity are the traits of character which develop in cooperation with these natural potentialities.

Increasingly, popular culture bombards us with a pair of very different claims.

One is that sexual difference is a "social construct" that has nothing to do with nature. Men can be house-husbands; women can seek service in the infantry. If they don't do so more often, it's only because they've been taught not to, not because their natures tend to pull them away from such decisions.

---

[*] "Men and Women: No Big Difference" (October 20, 2005), https://www.apa.org/topics/personality/men-women-difference.

The other claim is that sex differences aren't cultural, but natural—yet that nature makes mistakes. The sex "assigned" to a person at birth may be different than his "real" sex, so that he needs to "transition." This implies that the difference between masculinity and femininity is a natural given, though one oddly independent of the body.

We want to have it both ways. Sometimes the same people express both of these views, unaware of their inconsistency. The explanation is probably that both views embrace the same delusion: that manhood and womanhood can be whatever we want them to be.

According to the former claim, a man who accepts being a man can buck culture and "redefine" his masculinity, putting on perfume, layering on makeup, wearing a padded bra and women's clothing, and perhaps seeking the sexual attentions of other men. It's only culture—why not?

And according to the latter, a woman who wants to be a man, or who says her "real" self is male, can demand that her biological sex be changed by suppressing puberty, taking massive doses of hormones, cutting off her breasts, and removing her sexual organs. It's only a body—why not?

Plainly, some aspects of the roles men and women play really are variable. One of my nephews does most of the cooking in his home, because he likes it and is better at it. (He is a tough guy who also teaches martial arts.) In my house, my wife cooks and I clean up, but there was a period in our lives when it was more convenient to split cooking equally. My grandfather probably never entered a kitchen in his life. If he had tried, my grandmother would have chased him out.

Equally plainly, some people are uncomfortable with their sex. Psychologists used to call inappropriate discomfort with one's sex "gender dysphoria," a term that indicated the presence of a pathological mismatch between what a person is and what that person feels. That way of speaking made sense. Now, however, inappropriate feelings are taken to define reality, and if we say that they can't, then we are accused of lacking compassion.

As to the first observation—sex roles are culturally variable—there are limits to cultural variation. Psychological research shows that many sharp differences between the sexes hold consistently across countries, educational levels, ages, and years in which the research was conducted. And guess what? The contrasts correspond closely with traditional views of sexual differences—for example, concerning average levels of aggressiveness and nurturance. In fact, not only do we find the same differences everywhere, but we also find much the same views *about* these differences everywhere—even in countries like ours, where confessing that we hold them is slandered as prejudiced and retrograde. We can now confirm, by advanced sociological methods, that what everyone used to know without them is really true.[1]

As to the second observation—some people are uncomfortable with their sex—thinking one is a member of the other sex doesn't make it so. There is no scientific basis whatsoever for the idea that a biological man can be a woman, or that a biological woman can be a man, or that one can change into the other. All the evidence for "transmen" really being men, and for "transwomen" really being women, comes down to the mere fact that they say they are, or "feel" they are. How could a man who says that he "feels like a woman" know what a woman feels like anyway? He only feels what he *imagines* a woman would feel, or he feels a *desire* to be one.

We are embodied persons. Our minds are parts of what we are, but so are our bodies: They are not just containers or prisons for our true selves, but aspects of them. Indeed, the brain is indelibly stamped male or female.[2] Injecting hormones doesn't erase the stamp, and genital surgery doesn't affect it at all; sewing a penis on a woman does not make her a man any more than sewing a trunk on a man makes him an elephant. Brain physiologists tell us that large parts of the brain cortex are thicker in women than in men. Ratios of gray to white matter vary, too. The hippocampus, which plays a role in memory and spatial navigation, takes up a greater proportion of the female brain than of the male brain. On the other hand, a certain region of that same hippocampus is larger in the male. A variety of neurotransmitter systems work differently in men and women. The right and left hemispheres are more interconnected in female than in male brains, and the corpus callosum, which links them together, is larger. The amygdala, involved in emotion and emotional memory, is larger in men, but the deep limbic system, which is also involved in some aspects of emotion, is larger in women. Sex-related differences between the hemispheres exist for other brain regions as well, including both the prefrontal cortex, which is involved in personality, cognition, and other executive functions, and the hypothalamus, which links the nervous system with the endocrine system and is connected with maternal behavior. External circumstances, such as chronic stress, act on male brains differently than on female. Brain diseases also diverge in men and women. Even the neurological aspects of addiction differ between the two sexes.[3]

David Schmitt comments, "It is ironic that just when science is rapidly improving its fundamental understanding of sex differences and documenting the sometimes subtle ways that biology and culture interact, the progress has come under assault."[4] Yet there seem to be no limits to the delusion that manhood and womanhood are endlessly redefinable.

Some people want to have neither male nor female genitalia; others desire both kinds at once. Those who make their living by catering to their desires are happy to comply. One transgender surgery specialist explains in his website video, "If gender exists on a continuum, why then would my surgical treatments be binary? It doesn't make any sense to recognize that gender exists on a continuum but I'm only going to offer all male options or all female options."[5] A certified clinician who belongs to a committee revising the "standards of care" of the World Professional Association for Transgender Health goes even further: "Do we have to stick to penis and vagina norms? Can we have genitalia that looks like flowers or abstract sculpture? Can we have multiple? Can they be interchangeable?"[6]

Sexual activists and their allies now claim the existence of close to a hundred "genders." The application form for San Francisco's "Guaranteed Income for Transgender People" program (GIFT) offers ninety-five possibilities, including an option to fill in the blank if one's gender isn't listed.[7] The most imaginative option is "xenogender," which means a gender "that cannot be contained by human understandings of gender,"[8] although this raises a question: If it can't be contained by our understanding of gender, how do we even know that it is one? Supposed new genders are recognized seemingly every day. "Objectum sexuals," who are not on the San Francisco list, already have an organization to advance their interests.[9] A woman who "married" her briefcase after a five-year relationship says that although she has dated men and is "not against relationships with people," objects "really are better," and after all, "love is love."[10]

What gets onto these lists of genders is suspiciously arbitrary. For example, so far, "agender," "androgyne," "femme," "demiboy," and "intergender" are called genders, but "pedophile" is still a diagnostic category. The status of pedophilia may change at any moment, though, for pedophiles, too, have advocacy groups. Already some professionals call sex with kids "intergenerational intimacy" and propose calling people who enjoy fantasies of having sex with them "minor-attracted persons." As one scholar-activist writes, "From my perspective, there is no morality or immorality attached to attraction to anyone because no one can control who they're attracted to at all."[11] Even so, one wonders why "sadist" and "autoerotic" aren't on San Francisco's list, or why its GIFT program lists "aggressive" as a gender, but not "nasty bully"— or are they the same? Another great candidate is "adulterosexual," for do not many philandering husbands defend their infidelity by saying, "I was born this way"? Maybe they too should be eligible for stipends.

Sometimes activists quarrel over what is and isn't a gender. Wikipedia laments that "fictosexuals," who are sexually attracted to fictional characters, have not only "been marginalized or concealed in societies that adhere to the norm of sexual attraction to human beings," but "also face prejudice from the LGBT community" because "fictosexuality is often thought of as a preference" rather than a gender.[12] It seems that decisions about what counts as a gender reflect merely the degree of respectability each kind of sexual self-assertion has managed to attain. In our day, sexual disorder is organized for battle.

According to a widespread view, even if gender ideology is deluded, people cannot help how they feel, and therefore the path of compassion is to reassure them that their feelings are all right. This makes no more sense than if a patient told his doctor that he wanted to be intoxicated all the time, and the doctor concluded that his drunken self must be his true self, so that it would be unkind to discourage his drunkenness. Or if he told his doctor that he felt like a fox (some do say this!), and the doctor concluded that he must really be a fox, so that it would be insensitive to deny his inner fox-hood. Suppose the man then had the frontal lobes of his brain cut out, his limbs surgically altered for running on all fours, and his skin stimulated to grow a furry pelt, and was left in the wilderness to live in a burrow and eat mice—living as what novelist Gene Wolfe calls a "zooanthrope." Would this make him a fox? No, it would only make him a cruelly damaged human being. In the same way, a woman who has had hormone treatments and sexual surgery to resemble a man will not be a man, but a cruelly damaged woman.

Unfortunately, delusion has widening effects. For a while, hospitals in New Jersey actually asked new mothers and pregnant women the so-called gender identity and sexual orientation of their babies.[13] Apparently that practice has ended, but laws in several states not only permit but instruct schools to hide the so-called gender identity of children from their parents.[14] Bills have been proposed to allow children as young as fifteen to be given powerful hormone blockers and even to have mutilating surgery without parental consent.[15] Orwellian news reports describe such abuse as "gender-affirming care."

Research shows that "transitioning" does not eliminate the very great problems of persons suffering from dysphoria about their sex—this despite popular media claims to the contrary.[16] An important large study finds that post-surgery, transitioners have "considerably higher risks for mortality, suicidal behavior, and psychiatric morbidity than the general population."[17] Another finds that contrary to widespread claims that gender-confused persons who don't "transition" are more likely to kill themselves, nevertheless, when other relevant variables are accounted for, "the suicide mortality of both those who proceeded and did not proceed to GR [gender reassignment] did not statistically significantly differ from that of controls. This does not support the claims that GR is necessary to prevent suicide."[18] Just as this book was going to press, the U.S. Department of Health and Human Services released a comprehensive 409-page review of the evidence concerning pediatric medical "transition," finding that evidence of benefit is "based entirely on subjective self-reports and behavioral observations, without any objective physical, imaging, or laboratory markers." On the other hand, there is a lot of evidence about possible harms, including "infertility/ sterility, sexual dysfunction, impaired bone density accrual, adverse cognitive impacts, cardiovascular disease and metabolic disorders, psychiatric disorders, surgical complications, and regret."[19]

Speaking of regret: One man who eventually had his "transition" reversed writes, "Nothing made sense. Why hadn't the recommended hormones and surgery worked? . . . Why wasn't I happy being Laura? Why did I have strong desires to be Walt again?"[20]

Today those who say such things are punished.[21] As another man who sought reversal of his "transition" remarks, "Overnight, I went from being a liberal media darling to a conservative pariah."[22] Within hours of the release of the HHS report, it was already slammed as a politically motivated "fever dream."[23] At the mention of anything so vulgar as a fact, mental barriers drop like barred gates at castle entrances.

Lunacy 15

Men and Women Don't Need Each Other

∾

*Men redundant? Now we don't need women either. Scientists have developed an artificial womb that allows embryos to grow outside the body.**

O ur oldest legends testify to the prototypical presence of both longing and resentment between men and women. Seeing Eve, who was taken from his side, Adam says, "This at last is bone of my bones and flesh of my flesh!" Yet after disobeying God, he tries to put the blame on her: "The woman whom you gave to be with me, *she* gave me fruit of the tree."[1]

In our bitterest moments, we tell ourselves that we don't need members of the opposite sex at all. R. L. Boyce sings the blues about a woman who is always stirring up strife,

I don't need, need no woman
T' shoot me down in the middle of the night

---

* Robin McKie, *Guardian* (February 10, 2002), https://www.theguardian.com/world/2002/feb/10/medicalscience.research/.

I don't want any more trouble
But she got trouble in mind[2]

With a strong dose of cognitive dissonance, Nina Storey croons,

I don't need no man to help me be strong
And I don't need no man to string me right along
'Cause he'll mess with your mind and he'll mess with
    your heart
Then he'll tell you he loves you right before he departs[3]

The poignancy of her lyrics lies in their oblique recognition that men and women *ought* to love each other, that they *ought* to help each other be strong. Otherwise, why be cast down when they don't? The tacit message of the song contradicts its overt theme.

An uglier example of cognitive dissonance is found in a taunt song by a well-known girl band I will not identify, the lyrics of which are supposed to be "empowering" to young women. Its idea of empowerment is a strange one. Members of the troupe pattern their performances on burlesque, prancing around in undergarments while complaining about men who want sex. Three different messages seem to battle each other in the lyrics. The first may be put a little less explicitly, "I'm free, because the one thing you can give me, I can give just as well to myself." The second, "I'm not free, because what I really want from you is love, and you won't give me that." The third, "I'm free, because I have the power to sexually excite you and then turn you down flat."

But what's wrong with independence? Why *do* we need each other? Because by themselves men and women are incomplete; they need each other to be in balance.

The first way we are incomplete is that we are procreatively incomplete. It takes men and women together to turn the great wheel of the generations. The joining of a man and a woman forges a link in the long chain that connects remotest antiquity with remotest posterity, beyond any ancestors we can remember, beyond any descendants we can foresee.

When I was a boy, my teachers taught me that men and women have different reproductive systems. This claim was grossly misleading, because actually neither sex has a reproductive system. The man has one half of a reproductive system, and the woman has the other. Neither half can function by itself. If we were speaking of breathing, it would be as though the woman had the lungs, the man had the diaphragm, and they had to come together to make a single breath. If we were speaking of blood circulation, it would be as though the woman had the atria, the man had the ventricles, and they had to come together to make a single beat.

Breathing and circulation aren't like that, but procreation is. To make a single new life, a man and woman must join as though they were a single organism. In fact the expression "as though" understates the case. They are separate organisms with respect to the functions of individual life, but they become one organism, "one flesh," with respect to the life of the species. No wonder sexual intercourse makes us think, "Nothing will ever be the same."

The second way we are incomplete is unitive. Each sex complements the other; both are needed to make a whole. They are naturally different, but in such a way that they balance each other's deficiencies. Just as the thumb and fingers need each other to take hold of physical objects, so the two sexes need each other to take hold of human life.

This is quietly but pervasively true even in everyday matters, apart from sexual joining. Not only would the world be far less charming and color-ful with only one of the two sexes in it; it would also be unhinged, because each sex is incomplete, deficient in qualities more fully present in the other. Although this is true in every dimension, it is most conspicuously true in the sexual union of the spouses and their resulting partnership as parents. This should not surprise us, because it is *for the sake* of that partnership that they have such different designs. How often husbands need their wives to explain things they might never have understood apart from feminine insight! It works in the other direction, too; though the blind spots of mothers tend to be different, they are sometimes present.

The fact that men can love their male friends, and that women can love their female friends, has confused us about this fact, because we assume that sex makes love better. No; sex makes *the love which it consummates* better.

Sex does not make the love of a brother and sister, of a father and daughter, of a mother and son, or of a teacher and student better. In fact, it damages, undermines, and destroys it, even if intense pleasure and feelings of connection make us believe otherwise. Sexual union consummates, completes, and makes better *that love for which it was made*, the love of the procreative partners. Outside of that context it wreaks havoc.

We have seen previously that men tend to be more outward-directed, while women tend to be more inward-directed. Outwardness prompts him to pursue her; inwardness leads her to make herself attractive to pursuit. Because outwardness and inwardness are complementary, the sexuality of a man and the sexuality of a woman balance each other. For example, he can certainly acquire the virtue of sexual purity, but she will probably have much more to teach him about it than he has to teach her. By contrast, when two men (or two women) sexualize each other, their sexualities are not mutually complementary, but mutually reinforcing. Outwardness may turn into the explosive promiscuity of men who mate men; inwardness into the implosive emotional dependency of women who mate women.

But there is more to the complementary differences of men and women than the differences in their sexuality. As we said earlier, men are better designed to protect the hearth, women to nourish the life around it. A wise father teaches his wife and family that in order to love you must be strong; a wise mother teaches her husband and family that in order to be strong you must love. She knows that even boldness needs humility; he knows that even humility needs to be bold. He is an animate symbol to his children of that justice which is tempered by mercy, she a living emblem of that mercy which is tempered by justice.

How dreadfully the popular culture gets all this wrong. A writer for a magazine targeting young women vitriolically brands the idea that the sexes need each other as misogyny or woman hatred:

> Now if your argument is, "Of course you need a man . . . how else you will give birth?", save it and brace yourselves, because we're about to drop a truth bomb that may shake your misogynistic world up. Studies and reports state that close to 40 percent of babies are born to single moms, and there's a very

good chance that percentage will rise as the stigma of being a single mother decreases. And if that's not enough, there's also the fact that, thanks to technology, you don't even need a man if you want to have a baby—all it takes is a trip to your nearest sperm bank![4]

True, all you need for conception is borrowed sperm. But doesn't the child have a right to be conceived in the loving embrace of his parents? And while it's true that a rising percentage of children are born to single mothers, why must we consider this a good thing?

Why should anyone *choose* to deprive her child of his father, and deprive herself of his help? Why miss the chance for that heightened personal intimacy which can only develop in a secure and exclusive relationship? Why risk the poverty which often results from having to provide for the child all alone? Why consign the child to a lifetime without a father's restraining influence?

That is, if she has any choice over whether he sticks around. She may *not* have a choice, and this is probably the greatest driver of the bitter refrain, "I don't need a man." One of the cruelest aspects of the sexual revolution has been the rise of the view that if a woman conceives and refuses to get an abortion, the baby is no longer the man's concern.

In the end, even embittered men and women long for each other too much to live forever like elephants, with the females forming the herd and the males staying on the outside except when looking for mates. How long it will take the awakening to come is up to us, but there will be a lot of soul-searching, lonely lives, and broken childhoods before men and women rediscover just how much they really need each other.

Yet how grand rediscovery can be! One would think the ontological gap between the two sexes would make it impossible for them to enjoy true communion. Actually it is just what makes communion possible, by enabling them to give themselves to each other. You can't give someone what he already has, but only what he doesn't have. The division and incompleteness of the sexes is also a blessing because it provides a *motive* for crossing that gap. Men and women desire communion with each other.

Of course there are other ways to use the sexual powers, ways which fail to bridge that wide canyon. For example, one way sinks a person still more deeply into himself; another attaches him to his reflection, like Narcissus. Both trap us in the dungeons of our selves. By contrast, the union of two opposite sexes makes it possible for a person to forget himself in care and sacrifice for someone who is truly and strangely Other. Dying, yet we live; losing ourselves, we find who we really are.

Our holiest traditions describe crossing the gap between man and woman as a foretaste of crossing the even wider gap between man and God. It is not for nothing that heaven is described as a wedding feast.

IV

Delusions About What It Means to Be Human

We do our research on man without knowing what man is. Indeed, we presuppose or claim we have proved that no human nature exists.

—James Schall, "On 'Catholic' Universities"

Lunacy 16

Each Human Being Has His Own Nature

∞

Perhaps with the advances of medical sciences, we will come to know for sure the reason for our actions. So in the future when people say, "How come you are transgender," we can say guilt free, "Because I was just born that way."[*]

"I couldn't help seducing my best friend's wife. It's just my nature."

"I'm a hothead. I admit it. I was born that way. Deal with it."

"You say I'm a liar, but I say you're a loser. I'm good at lying, and I play the game with whatever nature gave me."

Popular culture drums into us the theme that each person's nature is different. So far, we are oddly selective. The idea of a promiscuous nature is greeted much more warmly than the idea of an adulterous one. Still, if we can have different natures, then how can we be measured by the same natural law?

What's wrong with this delusion will take some explaining.

Traditionally, the term "nature" is used to describe at least three different

*   Brianna Austin, "Born That Way" *Transgender Guide*, https://tgguide.com/transgender-resources/articles/transgender-topics/born-that-way.

things that concern us. One is the cosmos we inhabit and of which we are parts. The second is the shared requirements for living a life good for human beings. The third is the particular characteristics of any given human being— say, my friend Norman.

That seems pretty simple, but already some things need to be clarified. Although I speak of inborn characteristics, I don't mean that we spring from the womb with such traits fully grown, like Athena from the forehead of Zeus. From childhood, Norman may have been attracted to beauty, but not everyone with an eye for beauty develops a discriminating taste. This works the other way, too. For all I know, Norman may have been born with a genetic predisposition to fly into a rage but has spent his life working to moderate his bad temper.

But wait. If it's *natural* to him to fly into a rage, then why *should* he moderate his bad temper? Be patient. All will be explained.

We can call these three "natures" universal nature, species nature, and individual nature. The fact that three different things are all called "natures" is at the root of our delusion that each person has his own nature, for as in the last chapter, a fallacy of equivocation is involved. Each person *does* have his own individual nature—but we do *not* each have our own species nature.

Consider the proverb "A man reaps what he sows." This is about universal nature. It counsels us that all actions, including our own, have consequences. Matters couldn't stand otherwise, unless the cosmos were devoid of cause and effect.

The particular ways in which the proverb applies to us have mostly to do with species nature—to which we now turn. Consider the moral precept "Be faithful to your spouse." This bears directly on species nature. It reminds us that we human beings are designed with a view to marriage and family. Unfaithfulness wrecks homes, sows bitterness among us, and deprives our children of their parents. To flourish, we must practice faithfulness; if we don't, our lives become empty; and the Author of our nature, who detests self-destruction, expects it of us.

Finally, suppose Grandma were to say, "Ever since Edwin was a little bitty boy, he's wanted to give people things. Why, I recall that when he was still in arms, he took his soggy old teething biscuit right out of his mouth, pushed it in my face, and tried to get me to take a chew on it, too." This is a description of Edwin's individual nature.

Notice that to say that little Edwin wanted to give people things from babyhood is not the same as saying that little Edwin was *generous* from babyhood. Generosity is a virtue. The virtue of generosity requires judgment, because it lies in a mean between giving what we ought to withhold, and withholding what we ought to give. Babies lack judgment. Without it, little Edwin leaned toward one extreme, just as another boy or girl might have leaned toward the other extreme. Both tendencies need to be guided and moderated.

The fact that our inclinations require such discipline results from our shared species nature. Let's return to that little hothead Norman again. For every single human being in the species, anger has the same proper function: to arouse us to the appropriate defense of endangered goods. For our own human fulfillment, then, we need to be angry sometimes—but only at the right times and in the right ways. As humans, it is bad for us to underdo it— but it is also bad for us to overdo it. The hothead overdoes it.

The ideas of species nature and individual nature have been around for a long time. Here is what the Roman thinker Cicero wrote about them:

> We must realize also that we are invested by Nature with two characters, as it were: One of these is universal, arising from the fact of our being all alike endowed with reason and with that superiority which lifts us above the brute. From this all morality and propriety are derived, and upon it depends the rational method of ascertaining our duty. The other character is the one that is assigned to individuals in particular. In the matter of physical endowment there are great differences; . . . so in point of personal appearance. . . . Diversities of character are greater still.[1]

What Cicero calls universal nature is what we have been calling species nature, because it is not universal to the whole cosmos, but only to the human species. Bearing this in mind, we see that he recognizes both species nature and individual nature. But Cicero also insists that all morality, propriety, and duty are based on species nature, which we share—not on individual nature, which varies from person to person. Otherwise there really would be a different moral law for every person.

The fact that morality is based on species nature rather than on individual nature is crucial. If I have a congenital illness, we should not say that I merely have a "different health" than other people, but my health is objectively disordered. From birth, it deviates from the standard at which nature aims for us all. In the same way, if I have, say, a congenital tendency to philandering, bad temper, or drunkenness, I do not have a "different virtue" than other people, but I have a defect. In this case it is my desires that are objectively disordered.

A congenital temptation to some vice is a misfortune, but not an excuse. I will just have to work harder than others to control myself, just as if I have a weak sense of balance, I will have to work harder than others to walk. I may hope that from compassion, my comrades will encourage my effort at self-control. But compassion does not mean coddling my fault and encouraging me to give in to my temptation.

Differences in individual temperament, of course, can be good or bad. Most can be *either* good or bad, depending on how we regulate them. An unusually aggressive person might make a better soldier—but he will still need to be able to refrain from brutality. An unusually perfectionistic person might make a better craftsman—but when he has done his best, he will still need to be able to say, "I'm finished." An unusually talkative person might make a better teacher—but he will still need to know when to shut up. Always, the cardinal consideration in determining what's right isn't individual temperament, but the shared requirements for attaining a life good for human beings.

So far I have been writing as though whenever people say, "I was born this way," they are never mistaken—they were always born the way they think. But depending on which traits we have in mind, the claim may be false. Alcoholism seems to run in families, and the National Institutes for Health maintains that genetics seems to account for about half the risk of becoming alcoholic.[2] However, according to a study by scholars at Harvard and MIT, which studied the genetic makeup of nearly a half-million people, the environment in which a person grows and develops has about twice as much influence on same-sex attraction as genetics has.[3] A number of genes might have small effects, but the "gay gene" of popular legend is imaginary.

But suppose I really was "born this way." Even when they do come from birth, individual natures aren't fates. If I say, "Since I'm a born drunk, you should let me have another drink," I am treating myself as less than I am, picturing myself as a primitive organism running on hard-wired, blind, unmodifiable instincts. Shouldn't we have more respect for ourselves than that? Even when we suffer unwanted desires, we are rational beings capable of choice, beings who can learn from experience and reflect on the purposes embedded in the human design in order to steer ourselves appropriately.

Isn't this a bit harsh? No one has complete control over his thoughts and desires! True. But the objector forgets two things.

In the first place, we don't have to do as our thoughts and desires bid us. When he began an affair with his live-in girlfriend's adopted daughter, Woody Allen notoriously remarked, "The heart wants what it wants. . . . You fall in love and that's that."[4] But that's *not* that. Even if my heart wants what it wants, it can't compel me to give it what is wrong. The old-fashioned name for wanting something I shouldn't want is "temptation"—something to be resisted.

And in the second place, it is hardly compassionate to tell people they have *no* control over their thoughts and desires, because actually they have a good deal. Perhaps I can't just turn off an unwanted thought, but if I ignore it instead of fondling it, it will eventually fade away. Perhaps I can't just stop having an unwished-for desire, but I can get out of the situation which provokes it, or even stay out of it in the first place.

That helps a lot.

Lunacy 17

Human Nature Is Merely Animal

❧

If you read the literature on how similar bonobos and chimpanzees are to humans, you'll see how much humans are just animals.[*]

If by saying that humans are animals, one means that we aren't incorporeal intelligences but embodied beings, then of course we are animals. We have mass and take up space. We eat, digest, and dispose of waste. We are born from our parents' carnal union, and we have children by joining with spouses of the opposite sex. All these and many other things connected with embodiment are true.

Not everyone is pleased about embodiment. Reflecting on our animal architecture, the Psalmist stands in awe, exclaiming, "I am fearfully and wonderfully made."[1] But an online book reviewer is disgusted by it: "The fact that I'm a squishy bag of water freaks me out constantly: Thinking

_____

*   Scott Porch, "Yuval Noah Harari's Quick Primer on How to See Into the Future," *Daily Beast* (October 12, 2018), https://www.thedailybeast.com/ yuval-noah-hararis-quick-primer-on-how-to-see-into-the-future/.

about how fragile and necessarily ad hoc my respiratory and circulatory systems are, contemplating the various fluids and other things my body excretes, and of course, sex. Corporeal existence is weird and sometimes very inconvenient."[2]

When people say that humans are animals, they usually mean that we are "just" animals, "nothing special," with "no claim to superiority," even morally inferior. That we are animals is simply true—but to say that we are "just" animals, one must ignore the staggering difference between the other animals and ourselves. Only we are *rational* animals. In calling us rational, I don't mean that we always act for good reasons. The world is well-stocked with fools. But unlike all the other creatures, we always act not just on impulses but for reasons.

Disregard of human rationality provokes a variety of disturbing responses. One response is to say that since we're nothing but animals, we may as well live like them. The Bloodhound Gang became famous for chanting, "You and me baby ain't nothin' but mammals / So let's do it like they do on the Discovery Channel." No animal has the imagination to devise perversions like those the group mimed in their video. Even if the group had mimed real animal behavior, it is literally impossible for us to live like animals.[3] Just by trying to do so, a human being is doing something which could never enter an animal's mind: to follow an idea of how to live. Animals have no idea of living like animals. They live the only way they know.

Another response is to say that that since there is nothing special about human beings, we are free to treat people like animals—or even to treat them worse than the animals we happen to find cute. For example, we shouldn't experiment with laboratory bunnies, but we *may* experiment with tissue from aborted babies.

Yet another is to say that that since we have no special dignity as human beings, we have no greater duty to behave well than the other animals do. An ironical sidelight is that people who think this way tend to project the way they would like to live onto some other species, then model their own behavior on how they would like to think that species lives. For example, people who are attracted to anything-goes sexuality like to spin fantasies about how carnal matters are managed among the "gentle bonobos." However bonobos really live, one may be sure that they are not asking which species *they* should imitate.

Finally, some say that since the only difference between us and other animals is that our cleverness makes us more destructive, humans should be wiped off the face of the earth to make room for the other species. I have met this idea among students. One would have thought people who embrace it would further the movement by committing suicide. Strangely, they seem to prefer other pastimes.

A Reddit user writes, "Humans are just animals. And this world is a jungle. This is the truth, but we can't say it out loud because it would destroy people's ideas and their ignorance would be shattered."[4] There is something quaint about saying out loud what supposedly cannot be said out loud. A great many people have been saying this particular thing out loud for a good many years. More than a century ago, in G. K. Chesterton's time, the notion was already stale. He wrote that if you leave off reading books which liken man to the brutes,

> you will observe that the startling thing is not how like man is to the brutes, but how unlike he is. It is the monstrous scale of his divergence that requires an explanation. That man and brute are like is, in a sense, a truism; but that being so like they should then be so insanely unlike, that is the shock and the enigma. That an ape has hands is far less interesting to the philosopher than the fact that having hands he does next to nothing with them; does not play knuckle-bones or the violin; does not carve marble or carve mutton.

He continues, "[T]he chasm between man and other creatures may have a natural explanation, but it is a chasm." We speak of wild animals, but only man is really wild. So this first superficial reason for materialism—our likeness to the animals—"is, if anything, a reason for its opposite."[5]

A Quora user writes, "I hate how humans are so arrogant. The [h]uman race say they are superior than [sic] other animals. Animals don't destroy the environment, animals don't have wars, and they don't waste their time taking selfies."[6] Far be it from me to encourage us fallen human creatures to pretend to lofty virtues. But as we say, the most dangerous things aren't the ones you don't know, but the ones you do know that just ain't so.

For in fact some animals are extremely destructive to their surroundings. According to the Center for Animal Health and Food Safety, "A plague of desert locusts, the most destructive locust species of all, can easily affect 20 percent of the Earth's land, potentially damaging the livelihoods of one-tenth of the world's population and seriously affecting food security."[8] And yes, some animals do have wars. During what is known as the Gombe Chimpanzee War in the 1970s, a large group of Tanzanian chimpanzees split into two different clans and fought. Primate researcher Jane Goodall documented how over four years, the Kasakela clan violently killed every single male in the Kahama clan. Previously she had thought chimpanzees "rather nicer" than humans.[8] No longer.

True, animals don't take selfies, but that is because they aren't sufficiently aware of themselves to be vain. The self-awareness which makes vanity possible is a human point of superiority, like the capacity to recognize vanity as a vice. That Sheila has little vanity is a mark of good character, but a snake isn't better than Sheila because it doesn't have any, any more than a tapeworm is worse than she is for invading her innards. One may as well praise a scorpion for not committing injustice, or a virus for lacking ingratitude. Such creatures don't rise to the level of moral merit and moral fault.

Another Quora user—perhaps thinking of pets—agrees with the previous one, saying we humans are "much less unconditionally loving than our fellow animals." This, too, is naïve. Our fellow animals are no more capable of love than of failure to love. Chesterton—not the writer this time, but a cat of blessed memory—was unfailingly affectionate, and I grieved when he died. But he did not love me. I did not fault him for this. To love someone is to will his true good, but Chesterton had no concept even of his own true good, much less mine. Rationality requires the ability to grasp universal concepts, but his mind was stocked only with particulars: *this* warmth, *this* meal, *this* bird. Indeed since he didn't possess the concepts of warmth *as such*, meal *as such*, or bird *as such*, even that way of putting it falsifies the picture. All he really knew was *this, this, this*! He knew what to do with these things—warmth, lie in it; meal, eat it; bird, catch it—but he didn't know that he knew. He associated me with pleasing experiences, but he was not capable of thinking, "This experience is pleasing." What was going on in his mind when I stroked him might better have been put, "Mmmmmmm."

I have sometimes been asked: Doesn't the fact that children raised by wolves cannot function in human society show that there is no distinctive human nature? The questioners are presumably thinking that if we did have a distinctive nature, then it wouldn't matter how we were raised, for we would do all the same things anyway: compose sonnets, write hymns, build temples, invent steam engines, and have complex debates.

There really are said to have been a few cases of children raised by wolves, but the question is based on a flawed definition of "nature." It thinks of human nature as something like hardwired instincts, fixed patterns of action that don't need to be learned. If we use the term that way, then just because there are so few such patterns—just because we might learn to act all sorts of ways, or fail to learn to act in the ways expected—it will seem that we haven't any nature.

However, human nature includes much more than instincts. It is better to see it as a bundle of natural potentialities, distinct to humans, which must unfold for us to attain our full development and live well. In a properly human environment, they can unfold, but in a subhuman environment, they can't.

If there were no human nature, then children would flourish equally whether they grew up among humans, wolves, or ants. Among ants, they would thrive like ants; among wolves, like wolves; and among humans, like humans. What we find is that among ants, they can't function at all. Among wolves, they can function but not thrive, because natural human potentialities such as language and the desire for truth and beauty have no chance to develop in them. Only in a human society can they flourish.

We might say that our natural habitat includes not only things like food, water, air, dry land, and moderate climate, but also things like parents, friendship, conversation, good laws, and worship. Aristotle and Thomas Aquinas rightly say that man is "by nature" a social and political animal—"social" meaning that we live together and cooperate, "political" meaning that we try to provide for justice and take thought for the common good. It isn't that we can't live without such things. But without them, we can't live *well*. A good life for wolves is not a good life for us.

Lunacy 18

Everyone Is Evil— Or Deep Down, Everyone Is Good

∾

Because this is to be asserted in general of men, that they are ungrateful, fickle, false, cowardly, covetous, and as long as you succeed they are yours entirely; they will offer you their blood, property, life, and children, as is said above, when the need is far distant; but when it approaches they turn against you.*

> *A glass is good, and a lass is good,*
> *And a pipe to smoke in cold weather;*
> *The world is good, and the people are good,*
> *And we're all good fellows together.*†

How is it with us: Is human nature good? We seem to want a simple "Yes" or "No." Evidence for "No" is found in the fact that we often behave dreadfully. Priests who hear confessions will tell you that nothing surprises them. C. S. Lewis asked his readers whether they could go for a week without a base thought or urge. No? How about a day? Still no? How about an hour? I've asked the question myself, going as far as, "How about fifteen minutes?" No one yet has told me he could do it. Lewis himself didn't conclude that people are just plain bad—but many do. Commenting on the declining birth

---

* Niccolò Machiavelli, *The Prince*, trans. W. K. Marriott (1908).

† Anonymous.

rate, one writer describes the spirit of the age as "civilizational sadness," "a belief that we're just not good or that humans were a mistake."[1]

But on the "Yes" side, we do good things, too. Most of us have experienced kindness and friendship. Once past adolescence, most of us are deeply grateful to our parents. Isn't it good that we can recognize and desire good? In some sense, isn't it good just to be? And although we can do dreadful things, isn't it good that we are sometimes sorry and try to make amends?

Facts like these require a complex answer to the question "Is human nature good?"—but we want to keep it simple. The same urge to simplify rings through contemporary music. "I believe most people are good," sings country-western performer Luke Bryan, "and most mamas oughta qualify for sainthood."[2] Does this include the Hamas mamas who cheered on their sons in their mission of rape, mutilation, and beheading? Dave Gahan goes to the opposite extreme, singing that when he tells himself people are good, he's "fooling himself."[3] I've never heard a pop musician sing, "The answer is nuanced."

Traveling east, we find that classical Chinese thinkers also tended to offer a simple "Yes" or "No," and the lines their thoughts followed were much like ours. The two poles of opinion are well represented by Mencius, who thought our nature good, and Xunzi, or Hsün Tzu, who thought it thoroughly evil.

Mencius said, "Man's nature is naturally good just as water naturally flows downward. There is no man without this good nature; neither is there water that does not flow downward." By damming water you can force it uphill, and in the same way, he thought, man can be made to do evil, but that is not his nature. As evidence, Mencius offered our natural feelings: commiseration, shame and dislike, respect and reverence, and the feeling of right and wrong.[4] But can't we commiserate with the wrong people, be shamed into doing wrong, and reverence power divorced from justice? And although feelings are valuable data, can't they be mistaken? For the knowledge of right and wrong is not a feeling.

Criticizing Mencius, Xunzi said, "The nature of man is evil." Following natural feelings "will inevitably result in strife and rapacity, combine with rebellion and disorder, and end in violence." Therefore, "all propriety and righteousness are results of the activity of sages and not originally produced from man's nature." But why would we listen to these sages? Mustn't our nature contain at least a *desire* to be good? Weirdly, Xunzi answered that "[p]eople desire to be good because their nature is evil." Just as the mouth desires something flavorful because it doesn't have it, so a bad man desires goodness because he doesn't have it. Xunzi failed to see that a person who lacks goodness desires to have it *only because he recognizes the lack as a fault.* Surely this ability is something good. Besides, how have the sages become sages? Didn't they recognize truth and experience its attraction, and aren't those inclinations also good?[5]

Some Western thinkers have given more complex answers to the question of man's natural good or evil, but our desire to simplify their answers is so strong that we flatten out their nuances and read our own "Yes" or "No" into them.

For example, the Protestant reformer John Calvin is supposed to have taught that human nature is evil, but this greatly distorts what he said. He did think we have a pull toward doing wrong, an inclination from which nothing in our nature is exempt—neither our feelings, nor our thoughts, nor our will.[6] However, he also insisted that our good nature was not simply destroyed by this corruption. By nature we still have a foggy awareness of God, and even the pagans were "sufficiently instructed in a right course of conduct by natural law."[7] As he said against the Manichees, a sect which really did believe humans are naturally evil, "It is not admitted that there is any thing naturally bad throughout the universe; the depravity and wickedness . . . and the sins thence resulting, being not from nature, but from the corruption of nature; nor, at first, did anything whatever exist that did not exhibit some manifestation of the divine wisdom and justice."[8] All this is misunderstood not only by some of Calvin's opponents, but even by some of his followers, whose view of the inclination to sin is much more extreme than his.

Or consider Jean-Jacques Rousseau, who supposedly taught that human beings are naturally good and only society makes us bad. He did say we are naturally good, but he didn't mean what one might think. Before civilization, he thought, we were like animals, good only in the sense that we were capable of neither vice nor virtue. We would have found it painful to witness others suffer, but our discomfort with their pain wouldn't have prompted us to help, but only to flee from the sight.[9] Now that we civilized creatures have risen to being capable of vice or virtue, we mostly skip virtue and practice vice. Yet ever since Rousseau wrote, progressives have misread him as having held that if only civilization hadn't corrupted us, we would all be *virtuous*. At the very least, this raises the question of why naturally virtuous beings have invented such wicked civilizations.

We tend to flatten nuance in not only the works of philosophers and theologians, but also the findings of psychologists. Researchers who study babies have noticed that they have "glimmerings" of something which may later develop into virtue. For example, a baby may try to soothe another baby showing signs of distress by patting and stroking him, and infants as young as three months old respond differently to someone who helps another than to someone who hinders him. Researcher Paul Bloom describes such remarkable findings carefully, concluding that "moral judgment might have very early developmental origins." However, a science reporter who interviewed him put the matter much more strongly and carelessly: "Morality is not just something that people learn," but "something we are all born with."[10] This is misleading, for the research doesn't show that babies are naturally moral, but that they are born with a natural *push* toward morality, which is a very different matter. It's very good that small children like to see people helping others, but does morality dictate that no one should ever be hindered from doing anything? Besides, we all know that angry children not only soothe but also hit other children on occasion.

G. K. Chesterton jested that although some theologians deny it, the doctrine of original sin is "the only part of Christian theology that can really be proved."[11] I don't suppose he thought the story in Genesis can be proven. What he meant was nobody can fail to perceive that something in us is dreadfully askew—which is correct. But think: Evil cannot exist by itself. The only way to get something evil is to spoil something good. For example, we don't say that health is a disorder in disease, but rather that disease is a disorder in health. Likewise, we do not say harmony is not having enough dissonance, but rather that dissonance is not having enough harmony. Thus, if our condition is dreadful, there must be a wonderful of which dreadfulness is a perversion.

The conclusion to which I have been leading is that our nature is neither simply good nor simply evil, but created good and broken. It is bad that we are broken, good that we want to be fixed, good that we can mitigate some aspects of our condition, bad that we can't simply fix it. Moreover it is tragic both when we cynically fail to mitigate what we can—and when we indulge the utopian fantasy that we can fix what we can't.

For what's *wrong* with a simple "Yes" or "No"—apart from the fact that both answers so obviously ignore the fact that our good and evil are so entwined? It is that the error of a simple "Yes" or "No" is not merely intellectual. All too easily, both cynicism and utopianism, so contrary in their verdict on human nature, tend to the same possibilities: either gray tyranny, or red blood. Those in the camp of the cynics risk these outcomes because they have too low a view of human worth and good. Those in the camp of the utopians risk them because when they are up against the limits of fallen nature, they cannot stop pushing.

The milder forms of excessive pessimism and optimism are less dangerous, but they too have unfortunate results. When we are faced with evil, too dark a view of ourselves traps us in the dark den of despair, and too sunny an opinion blinds our dazzled eyes to what is wrong.

Curiously, we love nuance when our actions are at risk of being judged. How naïve, we say, to believe in a real right and wrong! How unsophisticated not to see that evil must sometimes be done for the sake of something good! No, those things aren't true, and in those ways, nuance is misplaced. But the condition of our nature really *is* complicated. We are not an unstained beauty, nothing so pure; nor a sheer ugliness, nothing so plain. We are a beauty in ruins, gleaming through a coating of muck. Anyone who misses the muck is making an enormous mistake. Anyone who misses the beauty is making another.

Lunacy 19

Human Nature Changes

&

The only thing that one really knows about human nature is that it changes. Change is the one quality we can predicate of it.[*]

The Communists thought they were creating a new human being, yet all they accomplished was the invention of new kinds of slavery. Alexander Solzhenitsyn's wry judgment was that "[h]uman nature, if it changes at all, changes not much faster than the geological face of the earth."[1]

Yet many, and not just Communists, think human nature so mutable that we shouldn't even speak of human nature. José Ortega y Gasset wrote, "Man is what has happened to him, what he has done. . . . Man, in a word, has no nature; what he has is—history."[2]

In the language of the street: Stuff happens. And that stuff is us.

This way of thinking was pioneered by Rousseau, who thought "perfectibility" the only fixed trait of our species. It was a strange term, because he

---

[*]   Oscar Wilde, "The Soul of Man Under Socialism," in *Collected Works of Oscar Wilde* (2007).

didn't mean that by nature we become perfect, but merely that by nature we change, with no obvious limit or direction. After a thousand years, a species of animals will be the same as at the beginning. By contrast, we might be—who knows?

It is probably even easier in our day to be taken in by the claim of continuous change in human nature than it was in Rousseau's, because we are so dazzled by our glittering technology. We may soon build cities in the ocean; we may raise our families on the moon. Yet such trivialities leave human nature untouched. Where we build communities hardly matters, compared with the fact that we still live in communities. Wherever we may raise families, we show no signs of no longer needing them.

In the same vein as these thinkers, Jean-Paul Sartre wrote, "There is no human nature. . . . Not only is man what he conceives himself to be, but he is also only what he wills himself to be after this thrust toward existence. Man is nothing else but what he makes of himself."[3] This claim does not even rise to the level of being wrong. It is incoherent, for human will is not something distinct from human nature, but a part of it. At best, then, when Sartre says we are whatever we will to be, he is badly expressing the idea that our will is greater than the *rest* of our nature. But in that case our nature matters after all, and our will is its best and noblest part—acquiring from its nobility a royal right to rule the rest of the kingdom. So if Sartre were to speak sense instead of nonsense, he would have to say that freedom is not freedom *from* the reign of human nature, but freedom of our nature's highest part to exercise reign over its lower ones.

So far as it goes, that principle is correct. Our highest part should rule! But what is our highest part? It couldn't be the will, as Sartre thinks, because the will does not know what to will. It would have to be the intelligence that directs the will. And now we come to the crux of the matter, for one of the highest functions of intelligence is to recognize the meanings and purposes embedded in the lovely array of the rest of the parts of our nature.

So many of our delusions concern things that are true in some sense or senses—but not true in the sense they are meant. That is the case here too. Taken in certain senses, of course human nature changes—but which senses?

Sometimes when people say human nature changes, they mean merely that humans are adaptable. Sure we are. In human beings, even behavioral predispositions are nothing like fixed, hard-wired ways of acting. But to say that adaptability shows that human nature changes is careless thinking, for adaptability is one of the permanent features of our nature—and we have others.

Others who say human nature changes mean merely that individual character changes. I may become more patient (or less), more imaginative (or less), or a better father (or a worse one). Or they mean that the frequencies with which particular traits appear may also vary a little, whether between population groups or over time. For example, it's not impossible that the average level of aggressiveness might rise or fall a bit—although there are probably limits to such variation. For example, if aggressiveness increased enough, it seems likely that the most aggressive males would die off in wars, so that the average level of aggressiveness dropped back to the norm.

Unfortunately, when people say human nature can change, they usually mean something quite different than any of these things. They mean there can be changes in what human nature is *aimed at*—alteration in the natural conditions for our dignity and well-being. The problem with this supposition is that these conditions are not merely incidental to us, like what color hair we have. They define us. And because they do, it is hard to conceive what it could even *mean* to say that they could change. We can imagine a red-breasted robin changing to an orange-breasted robin, because it would still be a robin. But we can't speak of a robin changing to an ox, because the robin would no longer exist. An ox would have taken its place.

Granted, the conditions we need for our flourishing are often violated. For example, slavery was once much more common than today (although there is a lot of it in our time, too). But slavery was not practiced in previous eras because in those times people needed chains to live well. Nor was it abolished because we changed, so that now, all of a sudden, we live better *without* chains. Beings of our kind have never lived well under slavery. Should there ever come a day when creatures descended from us need to be enslaved in order to flourish, the correct judgment won't be that human nature has changed, but that those creatures are no longer human beings.

I commented that those who say human nature can change usually mean that the natural conditions of human flourishing change. Translated into precepts, these conditions are the natural moral law. In this connection, it is worth mentioning that neither Rousseau nor Sartre had much truck with the natural moral law. Rousseau fathered a string of five illegitimate children, dropping each one off at an orphanage at birth. With his paramour, Simone de Beauvoir, Sartre sexually groomed and exploited numerous young girls and women, some of whom were their students, some of whom they both bedded, and some of whom described themselves afterward as used and traumatized. In general, a theory is not invalidated by its originator's behavior, but in this case we can at least say that the theories of these three thinkers provided excuses for their dreadful conduct.

Let's think a little more about the conditions for human flourishing. In the classical way of speaking—I have in mind such thinkers as Aristotle, Cicero, and Thomas Aquinas—the concept of human nature means more than just "things about us," such as having two eyes, two legs, and a gut. It means especially what counts as a good human life. All sorts of things about us could change without the conditions for a good human life changing. Any list of the most important dimensions of a good life for beings like us should include the following:

- We are social beings. For us, a good life isn't good unless we can share it with others. A good life without love, friendship, and communities is unthinkable.

- We are marital and sexual beings. Not everyone must marry, but we know our mates and enter partnership with them. Each sex is incomplete in ways only the other sex can balance.

- We are family beings. A husband and wife hope for children, and the relationship of their children with both parents—even with their surviving grandparents—is central to their well-being. The family is where we first learn sociality.

- We are moral beings. This means not that we always act morally, but that it isn't even possible for us to act badly without making moral excuses. So necessary and inescapable to us is moral reasoning that we think in terms of the right and the good even when we fool ourselves that evil is in some way good, or wrong in some way right.

- We are conscientious beings. We experience not only shame, as some of the other animals do, but guilt: an interior judge which weighs what we have done, and which we experience as the voice of God. Conscience is not just pumped in from outside. Even moral instruction builds on what is there already. Just as a child of the age of reason believes two plus two make four, not just because we tell him so, but because he can see that they do, so he knows he shouldn't pull sister's hair, not just because we teach him the Golden Rule, but because in it he sees something true.

- We are political beings. We seek not only the private but the common good, and despite such perversions as racialism, we believe that our shared life should be conducted with justice, according to what each person deserves. We enact laws and develop institutions to try to make sure this is the case.

- Finally, we are rational beings. Not only do we deliberate about our actions, but we seek knowledge. Knowledge includes not just brute facts about things, but the meanings of these facts and the connections among them—including the highest truths, and especially the truth about God. Moreover, we cooperate in searching these things out and try to pattern not only our individual but our shared lives on them.

Rationality could have been listed first, but I put it last because it colors everything else. We follow our natural inclinations neither automatically, like plants, nor instinctively, like the other animals, but with our minds. Thus, although we share many inclinations with other creatures, in us they are transformed by understanding and illuminated by rational meaning. Whatever marriage may have in common with mating, whatever friendship may have with the companionship of beasts, whatever human society may have in common with a herd, hive, or pack, among us these things are more and different.

Moreover, the other animals seek satisfaction, but we desire happiness. They seek to quench their desires, but we seek to flourish in a meaningful way which only a rational creature can conceive. We want our lives to make sense.

So long as humans endure, these things will endure, because they are what humanity means. If they cease, then we do.

Lunacy 20

We Can Transcend Human Nature

∾

We are going to become one with God. We are going to have almost as much knowledge and almost as much power as God. Cloning and the reprogramming of DNA is the first serious step in becoming one with God.[*]

For you have but to follow and as it were hound nature in her wanderings, and you will be able when you like to lead and drive her.[†]

It might have been a line from Dr. Seuss: Oh, the things we can be! At an assembly introducing freshmen to the academic majors, a scientist at my own university excitedly discussed the possibility of uploading our minds into computers, holding out the prospect as a reason for majoring in physics. Who wouldn't want to get in on the ground floor of something like that?

I wonder if the fellows who dream of machine futures ever ask, "Who writes the program?" Suppose someone displeased the programmers, or, if the virtual "reality" were consensual, then displeased the majority. Could

---

[*] Richard Seed, quoted in "Human Cloning Efforts," Joe Palca (reporter) and Bob Edwards (host), *National Public Radio*, Morning Edition show, Science Section (January 7, 1998).

[†] Francis Bacon, *De Augmentis Scientiarum* (1623).

he be punished with an eternity in virtual hell? Besides, even if my virtual self were still a *self* (a dubious proposition), it wouldn't be *this* self. The consciousness mediated by my brain would have died, or, more precisely, been murdered. What was running on the software would be a copy.

Uploading ourselves into computers is too far-out for most people to take seriously, but it is only one version of a surprisingly popular dream. Transhumanists don't just propose *restoring* natural function, for example filling cavities and curing colds. They propose *altering* human function with nanotechnology, biotechnology, and the cognitive and information sciences: Translated, this means drugs, chemicals, brain implants, psychological conditioning, and genetic manipulation.[1] The idea is that even if there is a human nature, it's obsolete. We can kick away the ladder by which we evolutionarily climbed, "direct our own evolution." Everything will be as we decree. There will be no limits—and abolishing limits *always* increases liberty and happiness.

But when we say "we" will make nature better, who is "we"? For whom will it be better? And since our former nature will have been abolished, by what standard will the change be judged?

Some transhumanists imagine the desired alterations being driven by consumer choice. Others imagine them as being directed by the powerful. Proponents of the former scenario ask you to suppose that your children are the only ones in school without brain implants for concentration on tests. You wouldn't want them to fall behind, would you? Already, self-dosing with ketamine, LSD, and "magic mushrooms," supposedly to free up the mind, is so widespread among the Silicon Valley elite that coming to work stoned is called "California sober."

But the consumer-choice scenario is just a way to open the door to the authoritarian one. We could release pheromones in the office so that file clerks never got bored, or down on the factory floor so that assembly line workers never wanted to go on strike. We could manipulate miners so that they preferred the heat and dark. As two promoters of the hoped-for revolution write in the *Wall Street Journal*, "Even if parents don't invest in brain implants, the military will." Challenging reluctant readers, they ask, "Who could blame a general for wanting a soldier with hypernormal focus, a perfect memory for maps and no need to sleep for days on end?" They add, "Spies might well also try to eavesdrop on such a soldier's brain, and hackers might want to hijack it." But this chilling prospect doesn't chill *them*. "The future doesn't belong to the fainthearted," they croon. "It belongs to the brave."[2] O brave new world, that has such altered creatures in it!

Such fantasies are no longer confined to science fiction. The Pentagon's Defense Advanced Research Projects Agency has been looking into them for decades. Chinese military publications speak of "genetic weapons." Russia is working on a "zombie gun" which could attack the brain directly to induce compliance. France is considering "augmented soldiers."

Transhumanism attracts big money. Among the ultra-wealthy who support various aspects of its agenda are: Raymond Kurzweil, Google director of engineering; Elon Musk, founder of Tesla and SpaceX; Peter Thiel, venture capitalist and founder of PayPal; Jeff Bezos, founder and executive chairman of Amazon; Larry Page, former CEO of Google and Alphabet, and one of the founders of the transhumanist think-tank Singularity University. Some influential scholars are also transhumanists, notably Nick Bostrom of Oxford's department of philosophy.

But why be so gloomy? If only we tamper with ourselves, couldn't life be more to our liking? Everyone could be smarter, stronger, and more musical. No one need become depressed, even if he had something to be depressed about. No one need suffer pangs of conscience, no matter what he had done. No one would ever have to be a square peg in a round hole, because we could trim off his corners until he fitted. No one need go mad from not knowing the meaning of his life, for our minds could be readjusted so we thought we knew already, or just didn't care. War would end, because nations would peacefully submit to whatever their programmers decided. We could be anything, perhaps even different things at different times. I will be a man this year, but a woman next year, a hermaphrodite after that, and perhaps, for a while, a Cocker Spaniel. Reality must bow to my choices.

So far, most people with whom I speak are still horrified by such proposals as the "enhancement" of soldiers so that they will be incapable of disobeying orders. Not many are attracted by such prospects as grafting in genes for chimpanzee muscles to make us stronger. Somewhat greater numbers experience a dark fascination with the idea of living twenty-four hours a day in virtual reality, although they are conflicted about whether what seemed real would be *really* real. But these are sideshows. I suspect that for most people, the real draw of transhumanism is the prospect of liberation from mortality.[3]

People who want to live forever rarely ask hard questions. The question I find most troubling about the prospect of that sort of immortality is, "How could we endure a world without the laughter of children?" For the abolition of death would also require the abolition of birth. My students are not much moved by this question, perhaps because their lives have so little room for the laughter of children even now. Contraception has brought us a world which is "sex-positive" but children-negative—or in which children are just a lifestyle enhancement.

Occasionally I hear the suggestion that "if only we live forever, we will have time to become perfectly virtuous!" No, virtue isn't a function of sheer age, but of which habits we cultivate—and if we aren't becoming better, we are becoming worse. Granted endless years in this life, a person who hasn't yet learned kindness by the age of threescore and ten will probably just go on becoming nastier.

More often, I hear suggestions to *make* us more virtuous by tweaking our genes. I recently read a technothriller in which humanity almost comes to an end because someone decides to play God, trying to implement an involuntary, virally transmitted polygenetic hack in order to make the whole human race smarter. What could go wrong? A lot. The first few supergeniuses try to kill each other. To his credit, the author realizes that we don't have an intelligence problem, but a virtue problem. Unfortunately, as the plot moves along, he and his character reach the wrong conclusion: We just need to play God *better*. For he concludes that we really do need a genetic hack, not to upgrade intelligence, but to feel more compassion.

A novel isn't an ethics treatise, but novels often encapsulate widespread errors. Yes, compassion is a virtue, but the author falls into the sentimentalist fallacy, viewing it as a feeling. But virtuous people don't just feel *more* of something. Virtue requires feeling the right things, for the right reasons, toward the right people, on the right occasions, to the right degree. Conceivably, a genetic hack might make me feel sympathy more intensely. What it couldn't do is make me more virtuous. It may even make me less. Feeling so much sympathy that I am unable to punish the convicted mass murderer doesn't make me compassionate; it makes me a ninny.

How has it come about that we have at last become so confused about what a nature is that we have come to believe we can invent one? I don't suppose transhumanists could achieve what they desire. I do think they might irretrievably damage us by trying. Their technologies, so-called enhancements, and so-called therapies would not enable man to transcend himself, but only to ruin himself.

If we throw out the natural conditions for human flourishing, we have no reason to do anything at all—or *not* to do anything at all. We have no more reason to feed the poor than to starve them, no more reason to champion justice than tyranny. We have no further reason to live—but neither have we reason to commit suicide. For we have "progressed" beyond the only standard by which progress can be distinguished from regress. Nothing remains but meaningless turbulence in obedience to *somebody's* whim.

Like the sorcerers of another day and time, the enchanters of our own time believe that freedom depends not on humanity, but on power. Just as we seek to subject glass, steel, plastic, and livestock to our will, so we suppose that we will be freer if only we can bend our own nature to our will. But regarding our bodies, our minds, and our sexes as *made things*, like television sets or digging machines, does not make us freer, but enchains us.

Every artist knows that to make beautiful things he must honor the laws of his medium, whether paint, stone, or sound. This is also true of the artistry of living, in which the medium in which our lives are etched is our nature. Demanding liberty to get outside our humanity is like blue wanting liberty to be red, odd wanting liberty to be even, or vegetable wanting liberty to be mineral. It is like demanding that our thirst be relieved, but by some means other than drink, or wanting our sickness done away with, but by some means other than cure.

Our nature is not a fetter, but a lovely gift. It is the substance of our liberty as finite creatures.

V

Delusions About What Is Real and Unreal

And since man has lost the true good, everything can appear equally good to him, even his own destruction, though so opposed to God, to reason, and to the whole course of nature.

—Blaise Pascal, *Pensées*

Lunacy 21

Reality Doesn't Have to
Be Logical or Make Sense

∞

*Twice two makes four seems to me simply a piece of insolence. . . . I admit that
twice two makes four is an excellent thing, but if we are to give everything its due,
twice two makes five is sometimes a very charming thing too.* *

I once remarked to someone, "Did you realize that you've just taken an incoherent position? You say truth *can't be known*, all the while supposing that
you know it can't."

"I guess I am being incoherent," he replied. After thinking a moment
longer, he said, "That's all right. The universe is incoherent, and I don't need
to have meaning in my life."

Once upon a time I would have argued with someone like that. My
mistake in those days was to take such statements at face value instead of as
the smokescreens they are. They are ways to hide from something.

By this time, though, I had figured that out, so I said instead, "I don't
believe you. You know as well as I do that the longing for meaning and

---

*   Fyodor Dostoyevsky, *Notes from Underground* (1864).

coherency is deep-set in every mind. So the real question is this: What it is that is so important to you that you are willing to give up even meaning and coherency to have it?" It took him several minutes to recover and get back in the groove of empty cleverness.

On another occasion a postmodernist candidate for a university professorship in political philosophy offered me two examples to show that inconsistent realities can both be so at the same time. The first: A ball that is black on one side and white on the other is both white and black. The second: Every curve is both concave and convex.

I replied that although it would be contradictory to say that a ball is both white all over and black all over, there is no contradiction in saying that it is black on one side and white on the other—and that although it would be contradictory to say that a curve is both concave and convex viewed from the same side, there is no contradiction in saying that it is concave viewed from one side and convex viewed from the other.

She thought this view of things naïve, and when the faculty met to decide on hiring her, they were comfortable with her thinking. One said to me, "Haven't you ever heard of fuzzy logic?"[2] The candidate got the job.

The idea that reality is illogical is incoherent. One can't even argue that it is true, because logical arguments presuppose that reality is logical. That is, even to give a reason for thinking reality illogical, one has to assume that it isn't. Even so, the delusion is common and resilient.

Consider the social media remark, "Math is actually not universal. Treating it as such upholds white supremacy."[2] It's easy to laugh, but the author of the tweet is a math teacher, and this sort of thing is actually taught in some public schools. Or consider the tweet: "2+2 in #Theology can make 5. Because it has to do with #God and real #life of #people."[3] This was posted by theologian and papal confidante Antonio Spadaro, who was defending certain statements against critics who had pointed out that the statements contradicted the moral doctrine of the Catholic Church.

Motives for embracing incoherency are often obscure. I am mystified by the belief that mathematical reasoning upholds white supremacy, or that illogic serves black liberation. Sometimes, though, the motives for embracing incoherency are clear enough. If one wishes to deny something without admitting that one is doing so, the easiest way is to say that two inconsistent statements can both be true.

As we have seen, every delusion contains a grain of truth. There can be no *valid* reason to hold that reality is illogical—but there can be reasons. What does the delusion have going for it? What genuine truths might make someone feel justified in claiming that nothing has to make sense?

Some people think reality can be illogical because not everything can be easily captured in logical formulae: "Not everything is black or white." That's correct, but it doesn't follow that black can be white. This particular excuse for illogical thinking is trotted out when people don't like an argument, but they can't find anything wrong with it. Once in class, after I had explained the concept of a sound argument, a student raised his hand and asked, "What if the premises are true and the reasoning is valid, but you *just know* the conclusion is wrong?" I answered, "Then you change your mind."

Other people plant their flag on the fact that a great many generalizations have exceptions. That point is also correct, but they misapply it. For example, they may say that taking a gun from the hands of a killer is a case in which "stealing is not stealing." But no, stealing is *unjustified* taking. Justified taking—for example, imposing a fine for reckless driving, confiscating stolen property in order to return it to its rightful owner, depriving a violent and angry person of the means of doing injury—these things are not stealing at all, much less "stealing that is not stealing." The effect of this particular confusion is to encourage us to think that classifications are arbitrary, so that whenever we don't want them to be, murder isn't murder, cheating isn't cheating, and injustice isn't injustice.

Still others consider it a crushing argument against logic to point out that man does not live by logic alone. He doesn't, but if I may make a logical point: From the fact that we need more than logic, it doesn't follow that we don't need it. With logic it is much the same as with water. A man who has only water to drink is in a sorry state, but a man who does not even have water is dead.

And finally, some think the world is illogical because it is full of paradoxes.

A paradox is a pair of insights, each of which seems to be true, but each of which seems to contradict the other. The key word is *seems*, for two things that seem inconsistent might not be. For example, as Chesterton points out, there is no intrinsic incompatibility between happiness for others and for myself, though there may seem to be. Appreciating paradoxes is indispensable to sanity, but it isn't sane to leap from the possibility of paradox to the possibility that logical contraries can be true in the same sense at the same time.

It is hard even to know what someone *means* in claiming it is false to say a meaningful proposition can't be both true and false. In that case, mightn't the statement that propositions *can* be both true and false *itself* be both true and false? What would the denier make of that? One denier did offer me an answer: "Wait—what?"

Moreover, it has been known for centuries that from a contradiction, literally anything can be shown to follow. For example, if snow is white, and also snow is not white, then it follows that God exists. Here is how it works: Assume both that snow is white, and that snow is not white. That snow *is* white implies that *either* snow is white *or* God exists. But given this, and that snow is *not* white, it follows that God exists.

But from the same contradiction, it follows that fairies like ice cream. And that God *doesn't* exist. And that fairies don't eat at all. And that it *isn't* true that snow is white. Any claim whatsoever can be inferred. This calamitous result is sometimes called "explosion." It would seem that whenever there is an inconsistency in a system of propositions, the game is up. From there on, everything is nonsense.

Some logicians have developed so called paraconsistent logics, which tolerate inconsistencies. Even here, though, the reason is not that inconsistent statements actually can be true in the same sense and at the same time, but that it may be helpful to insulate the rest of a system of propositions from so-far-undiscovered inconsistencies—to cautiously keep using the system while trying to find and uproot them. This is akin to what computer programmers do when they try to keep their programs from crashing, even though those programs inevitably still contain some bugs.

The idea that reality can be illogical takes another form, too: Claiming that meaningful propositions can be something *other than* true or false. Can't they? It may seem that they can. After all, don't we say there are half-truths?

We do say that, and some logicians have even tried to formalize such ways of speaking. But they should never be taken literally. The claim that something is half true may mean many things, but never that.

For example, if I call the statement "The cloth is white" half true, I probably mean that "The cloth is gray" is completely true. If I call "Calico cats are even-tempered" half true, I probably mean that half of calico cats are even-tempered, or perhaps that calico cats are even-tempered half the time. If I say, "Sam is a dog" is half true, I probably mean that it is figuratively true (he behaves badly) but literally false (he is human). Or take the statement "This here is a heap of sand." If I call it half true because the term "heap" is so vague, I probably mean, "Gee, there sure seems a lot of it to me"—and that is just true, for it does!

Or I might call the statement "Mary is a doctor" half true because it is true in one sense; or that "Pegasus is a winged horse" half true because he exists only in the story; or that "The car is in the garage" half true because half of it is in the garage; or that "A child is an adult" half true because the child has traversed half the distance toward adulthood. We could continue this. But in no case whatsoever do we actually encounter a meaningful statement which is neither true, nor not true, but something in between.

So the figure of speech "half true" is merely an amusing, ambiguous shorthand for something that can be expressed more clearly in a different way. It does not describe what is actually the case. It doesn't show that some things are half real—any more than limericks about things that taste like the number seven show there are things that taste like the number seven.

Reality is always *some* way, even if we don't know which. To deny this fact is only to give ourselves excuses for not facing it.

Lunacy 22

Each Person Has His Own Reality

❧

Student A: So if someone decides he's a refrigerator, then he's a refrigerator?
*Student B: It wouldn't be like that. He would have been a refrigerator from birth.**

I have a very hard time understanding how anyone can tell me what I should believe or what is right," writes an internet "influencer." "We don't even have the same realities."[1]

If we have different realities, then I wonder what happens if, in my reality, we *don't* have different realities. I suppose the influencer would say "So what—we do in mine!" But if she thinks our realities are different, then how does she acquire the right to say that her view of things is true? Yet since I think our realities are the same, I can still say that her view of it is false.

All sorts of nonsense are found on the web, and one should not take internet influencers very seriously. But the way this influencer thinks is widespread; that's why she's an influencer. Philosophers recognize such thinking

---

* Anecdote related to me by a student about a discussion in one of his classes.

as incoherent. If it's true, then by that fact, it can't be true. This doesn't stop some philosophers from taking up similar ways of thinking.

The idea that each person has his own reality is treated as an article of faith in some schools of social work and counseling. When a Jungian psychotherapist with whom I chatted one day explained that one of her guiding axioms was everyone has his own reality, I was puzzled. What could she mean? The conversation went something like this.

Me: "Do you mean that each person has his own *opinion* about what is really real, even though he may be mistaken? For instance, you may think Frances lives in San Antonio, but I think she lives in Austin?"

Her: "No, I mean a lot more than that."

Me: "Then do you mean that certain facts may be true *for* everyone, but not true *about* everyone? For instance, for both of us it's true that you're married to John, and for both of us it's true that I'm married to Sandra, but I'm not married to John, and you're not married to Sandra?"

Her: "No, you're not getting it."

Me: "Then are you suggesting that reality *seems* different to different people? For example, Frank might have meant to pay Ann a compliment, but Ann took it as a slight?"

Her: "I'm afraid you're still missing my point."

Me (running out of ideas): "Are you pointing out to me that some aspects of reality may depend on what I think? For example, If I wish Sandra would kiss me, then it's true for both of us that I have that wish?"

Her: "No, no. Each person has *his own* reality. Reality is *not the same* for you and me."

Me: "Then it seems to me you're saying that we live in different universes."

Her: "Now you get it! We do!"

Me: "How could that be? In that case we wouldn't even speak with each other, but here we are in conversation."

Perhaps I was too persistent. By this time she was quite irritated with me. We dropped the subject and spoke of other things. Not, I'm afraid, for very long.

The grain of truth in the view that each person has his own reality is that each of those four things I thought the lady might mean are true—but true, mind you, for everyone. These grains of truth may tempt us to believe we have different realities, even though there is only one.

For yes, we have different opinions about what is real, but a true opinion is one that corresponds with how things really are. And yes, some facts about different people really are different, but they are really different for both of us. And yes, things really seem different to you and me, but that doesn't make them so. And yes, my very thoughts may cause certain things to be true about me, but they are true about me for you, too.

This isn't difficult. Why do we give in so easily to the temptation to believe we have different realities?

Partly to make excuses. If we have different realities, then perhaps we have different moralities—a delusion we dismissed in Lunacy 2. How convenient that would be. Stealing might be wrong for you but right for me. Sleeping with my neighbor's wife might be wrong for me but right for you. As a few of my students have suggested, genocide may be wrong for our country but right for another one.

Old-fashioned moral relativists were pikers. They tried to say that we can "create our own values," even though we live in the same universe and it is already here. The first of the new-fashioned moral relativists, Friedrich Nietzsche, realized that in order to make good on the claim that we can create our own values, we would have to be able to create our own realities. Thus he held that there *is* no objective reality, but only interpretations of realities—and since different interpretations of reality are inherently at war, in the end there is only will to power. But of course Nietzsche was incoherent, too. To say there "is" only will to power is to say that there is an objective "is" after all—but if there is one, then will to power can't be all there is! Nietzsche couldn't solve this problem. He didn't try. He merely laughed at rational solutions, considering them crocks. Of course, to say they *are* crocks is to claim something about reality. We can't get away from making such claims.

Another possible explanation for the fact that we give in so easily to the temptation to believe we have different realities is that we want to escape from the one we are in. Have I made a mess of things? Then I imagine a reality in which I haven't. Am I unwilling to stop doing things that make me miserable? Then I imagine one in which I don't have to. Am I unwilling to repent the wrong I did my former friend? Then I imagine one in which it was all his fault. This fits in very well with the view of so-called pragmatist philosophers that truth is "whatever works." Presumably, if atheism "works" for Todd, but faith in God "works" for Anthony, then in Todd's universe there isn't any God, but in Anthony's there is. Impossible. Todd and Anthony inhabit the same state of affairs. Either God is or He isn't.

But wait. Hasn't the Great God Science now shown that we have different realities? So we're told, but no. Let's investigate the claim. One of its two main varieties trades on neuroscience, the other on quantum physics.

The idea that neuroscience shows that we have different realities depends on a pretty large fallacy of equivocation: using the same word for both reality itself and our perceptions of it. We do have different perceptions. A straight rod lying halfway in the water and half out of it will look bent to me, but if you pull it out, it will look straight to you. But this does not show that it is bent for me but straight for you: It only shows that water refracts light. To say that just because we have different perceptions, we have different realities, is like saying that just because I am at peace, the world can be at peace. Peace in the sense that a given individual is calm and content is not the same as peace in the sense that no armies are shooting at each other.

To illustrate such equivocation about what is real, consider a *Scientific American* article on the so-called "neuroscience of reality." Actually, the article has nothing to do with reality itself, but only with perceptions of it. The author confuses them. For example, he asserts that because colors are a mental representation of mixtures of wavelengths of light, "colors do not exist out there in the world." This claim is misleading, for light really does come in different wavelengths, and colors really are how humans experience those wavelengths. Of course the nonhuman parts of the universe don't have human experiences, but so what? It doesn't follow that our experiences aren't real.

Again, because our brains have to process sensory perceptions to put together pictures of our surroundings, the author claims that "if my brain is different from your brain, my reality may be different from yours, too."[2] This is more than misleading; it is absurd. How I picture our surroundings may be different than how you do, but we are in the same surroundings.

As to quantum physics, occasionally people claim that the possibility of inconsistent realities is proven by "Schrödinger's cat." I am referring to a famous thought experiment proposed by the physicist Erwin Schrödinger, in which a cat is locked in a box with a tiny bit of radioactive matter, along with a vial of poison gas which is connected via a relay with a Geiger counter. If a radioactive nucleus decays, the vial of gas is shattered and the cat dies. If it doesn't decay, no gas is released and the cat lives.[3]

Sometimes it is claimed that until the box is opened and the condition of the cat is observed, the cat is both dead and not dead. Not so. Until the box is opened and the condition of the cat is observed, *we simply don't know* whether it is dead or not dead—just as we wouldn't if the condition of the cat had depended on a coin toss instead. True, the *possibility* that the cat is dead coexists with the *possibility* that it is not dead, but this in no way suggests that the dead cat coexists with the live cat. It turns out that this was Schrödinger's own view as well! The one and only thing the thought experiment really shows is that events in the "little" world (like the decay of a nucleus) can have effects in the "big" world (like the life or death of a cat). And here is the point: *Even if the cat were alive in one universe and dead in another one*, it wouldn't follow that it can be both alive for you and dead for me, because we are in the same universe.

Although the predictions of quantum theory have proven highly accurate, the notion that we can have different realities is nonsense. Unfortunately, the more *outré* interpretations of what is going on with the imaginary cat receive more attention from science popularizers than the sensible interpretations do. Saying "quantum" today is something like chanting "abracadabra" in an age of superstition. It makes us expect something magical.

Yes, our brains are somewhat different. Yes, our perceptions are somewhat different. Yes, our circumstances are somewhat different. Like it or not, though, we breathe the same air and inhabit the same world. The sooner we admit the fact, the sooner we can deal with it.

Lunacy 23

Things Are Whatever We Say They Are

❧

If facts work in your favor, use them. If they don't (or you don't know them), then redefine the terms instead.[*]

The ideal subject of totalitarian rule is not the convinced Nazi or the dedicated communist, but people for whom the distinction between fact and fiction (i.e., the reality of experience), and the distinction between true and false (i.e., the standards of thought), no longer exist.[†]

W hat's in a name?

A 5'9" male Anglo interviewer from a policy institute had himself videoed speaking with students on the campus of the University of Washington. The exchange with one young woman went like this:

"If I told you that I was a woman, what would your response be?"

"Good for you! Yeah!"

"If I told you that I was Chinese, what would your response be?"

"I might be a little surprised, but I would be, like, good for you, yeah, be who you are."

---

[*] Jay Heinrichs, *Thank You for Arguing: What Aristotle, Lincoln, and Homer Simpson Can Teach Us About the Art of Persuasion*, 3d ed. (2017).

[†] Hannah Arendt, *The Origins of Totalitarianism* (1968).

"If I told you that I was seven years old, what would your response be?"

"If you feel seven at heart, then so be [it], good for you."

"So if I wanted to enroll in a first-grade class, you think I should be allowed to?"

"If that's where you feel, like, mentally, you should be even, I feel like there are communities that would accept you for that."

"If I told you I'm six feet, five inches, what would you say?"

"I feel like that's not my place—I was—like another human to say someone is wrong or to draw lines or boundaries."

Some students pushed back just a little. For example, one said the interviewer could be a Chinese woman, just not a 6'5" Chinese women. Another said the interviewer would have to explain *why* he thought he was a 6'5" Chinese woman—but then he would go along.[1]

Could it be that the students don't believe such things can be true, but merely want to avoid hurting the feelings of those who do? I think much more is going on. One day in class we were discussing the nature of marriage. Some students were puzzled: How could anything have a nature? As one student put it, "We can define things however we want." There you have it.

The same view plasters social media. A Reddit contributor posts, "Bro everything is arbitrary if we made it up and agreed upon it."[2] Though his grammar is a little hard to parse, his opinion is clear enough. Since words don't refer to actually existent things, we can use them to mean whatever we want to. Whatever we say, makes things so.

Besides, something more than not wanting to hurt feelings is going on when male rapists who say they identify as women are housed in women's prisons, when police and campus cops no longer apprehend men who invade women's lavatories, when female athletes are hounded for wanting to compete only with other women, or when they are scolded for not wanting to share locker rooms with naked men having erections.

People who do such things are not just trying to be tolerant. They believe reality itself is intolerant, reality the culprit, reality the persecutor. Reality must be punished, and all her cruel allies brought to heel.

In the idea that reality is whatever we say it is, there is a grain of truth, for there is a conventional element in meaning. For instance, we could have called north "south," or called south "north." Yet even distinctions like these are not simply arbitrary. Because of the rotation of the earth, it is convenient to distinguish north (toward one pole of rotation), south (toward the other pole of rotation), east (the direction of rotation), and west (the direction opposite rotation). Sure, we could have divided the horizon into three cardinal points instead of four, but it would have been extremely awkward.

Moreover, many aspects of how words divide up the world are not conventional at all. A "furry" who wants to be treated as a fox or unicorn is not really a fox or a unicorn but a human. A human being who by nature possesses the potentiality of fatherhood is not interchangeable with one who possesses the potentiality of motherhood. When we choose to pretend that things are otherwise, we quickly get into trouble with reality. I daresay even the person who says, "Treat me as a fox" doesn't want to be kept in a cage and fed kibble.

How could we ever have thought things are whatever we say? Several versions of the idea have long pedigrees. For example, according to a useful principle of intellectual thrift or non-extravagance, we shouldn't assume things that we don't need to assume. Sometimes this is called "Ockham's Razor," although William of Ockham was only one of many thinkers who proposed it. The Razor is a helpful and even indispensable principle, but it is often misapplied. Often, it is fallaciously used to argue that we should reject the belief that reality contains those enduring patterns which are called "natures" or "essences." According to this argument, such things are superfluous; it is much simpler to suppose that they don't exist. For example, the reason we call cats "cats" is merely that we have placed them in the set of things we do call cats, isn't it? So why must we assume some mysterious thing called cat nature, cat essence, or "catness"?

But wait a moment. *Why do* we place certain things in the set of cats, and not place others there? We don't call them cats because we have placed them in the set; we place them in the set *because they are cats*. We do it because they do all have catness. Dogs don't. So pushing essences out the door turns out to be harder than it looks. In fact, it's something like—well, in the common expression, herding cats.

Another confusion concerns the nature of truth itself. Classically, truth was held to lie in correspondence with how things really are. For example, the proposition that "snow is white" is true *because snow really is white.* Today this view is thought naïve. Why shouldn't we adopt another "theory of truth"?

The coherence theory takes truth to be whatever follows consistently from our assumptions. The grain of plausibility in this theory is that if our assumptions are true, then whatever follows consistently from them will also be true. But doesn't this beg the question? *Are* our assumptions true? What must *they* cohere with? The beliefs of someone who thinks he is Napoleon may cohere with each other, but they are mistaken. What they need to cohere with is what is actually the case.

The consensus theory takes truth to lie in whatever we *agree* to be the case. Something like this theory seems to lie behind the demand to criminalize so called misgendering: "If only we can force everyone to agree that a man can be a woman, *then it will be true.*" The grain of plausibility in the consensus theory is that something which is obviously true often does elicit consensus—but that is far from showing that consensus *just is* truth. Who is "we," anyway? If consensus means what everyone agrees to, then if I don't agree with the consensus theory, it isn't true. If it means what "my kind of people" agree to, then we are not describing truth, but only prejudice. If it means what powerful people agree to, then we are not describing truth, but only thought policing. And if it means what the people *best qualified to judge* agree to, then we are back to correspondence—because a well-qualified person is one who is likely to know what is really the case.

The pragmatist theory takes truth to lie in "what works." This time the grain of plausibility is that if we hold beliefs which don't accord with how things really are, things usually won't work. For example, the theory that marshmallows make good bricks doesn't work, because buildings made of marshmallows fall down. But if we say that truth *just is* what works, we have a problem. Suppose I ask whether the pragmatist theory of truth is itself true— whether it *works* to believe that truth is whatever works. Presumably, a belief "works" if it brings about what we desire. Then would the bank robber's belief "I ought to shoot everyone" be true because it enables him to take all the money? Suppose I ask *which criterion* of "what works" is the true one. A pragmatist would have to say "the true criterion of what works is the criterion that works." But this is merely circular.

G. K. Chesterton wrote, "There is a thought that stops thought." He didn't mean that someone who thinks such a thought falls into a coma, but that once he begins to believe it, he can hardly be said to be thinking.[3] The thought "Reality is what I say it is" stops thought, because it severs the correspondence between the mind and what is there. Strictly speaking, it can't even be rationally challenged, because it is a conversation stopper: It disallows the very possibility of challenge. I can't reach you by saying, "That's not a dog, that's a cat," since you think reality is whatever *you* say. I can't even say, "Reality is *not* whatever you say," since if you say it is, then it is. Between me and you lies a glass wall which lets sound pass, but not meaning. Nobody can reach you. You cannot learn anything. You must be lonely in there. And if your "I" becomes "we," it is merely a lonely crowd.

The length to which disconnection can go is shown by a former colleague who reasoned like this: (1) Every term is defined by its opposite—wrong as not-right, false as not-true. (2) Therefore, every statement *implies* its opposite. (3) Therefore, every statement contradicts itself. She could no longer believe that truth lies in correspondence with reality, for in her view there was no reality to which truth could correspond. Distantly echoing the idea that God is the standard of reality, she declared, "God is a liar."

These lunacies are not mere curiosities. They have real-world consequences. More and more, politicians, marketers, and activists lie, because they think words make truth. Less and less do people who have disagreements talk them out, because they no longer believe in an independent reality for their disagreements to be about. More and more, ordinary folk claim that right and wrong must have changed, because "we" have changed our minds about them. And we meet ever-larger crowds of desperate people whose ways of life are not "working" by any reasonable standard, but who nevertheless say, "It works for me."

Where does the Orwellian nightmare end? If we can say that an Anglo man is an Asian woman, a human is not a person, burning buildings is not rioting, racial segregation is racial inclusion, killing a child is reproductive care, raping and beheading is liberation, or surrounding and threatening persons who make videos exposing genocidal rallies is de-escalation—all of these claims are actually made—then it is child's play to say war is peace, freedom is slavery, and ignorance is strength.

Truth lies in conformity of the mind with what *is*. To betray this principle is to betray the mind itself, and turn traitor to the universe.

Lunacy 24

All That Exists Is Material

Thoughts are to the brain as the bile to the liver or the urine to the kidneys.[*]

The delusion that things are whatever we say they are gives such an inflated importance to the mind that one would think nothing existed but thoughts, or maybe words. Materialism swings to the opposite extreme: that nothing exists but matter and material bodies. If nothing but matter exists, it seems to follow that there is nothing but matter to care about: As one pop diva famously chanted, "[T]he boy with the cold, hard cash / Is always Mister Right / 'Cause we are living in a material world / And I am a material girl."[1]

"Matter is all there is" is so much taken for granted that the *Encyclopedia Brittanica* simply announces it as fact. Matter, it declares, is "material substance which constitutes the observable universe and, together with energy, forms the basis of all objective phenomena."[2] The phrase "together with energy" adds nothing because energy can be converted into matter.

---

[*]   Karl Christof Vogt, *Physiological Letters for the Educated of All Classes* (1847).

153

To say that "matter is material" is circular, of course. More commonly, matter is taken to be whatever has mass and takes up space. In this sense, dirt is matter, but the meaning of the definition isn't. Assuming that this is what the *Brittanica*'s editors have in mind, it seems that the meaning of their sentence could be neither observable nor objective—yet somehow they expect us both to observe it and accept its objectivity.

Perhaps they would say that the ink marks spelling out the words of the definition have mass and take up space. They do, but these marks are not the definition, but only a symbol of the definition. For suppose we switched to using pixels of light on a monitor instead of blotches of ink on paper. If the definition and its material representation are the same thing, then we have to say that since the representation has changed, the definition has changed. But it hasn't. The definition is immaterial, independent of the matter symbolizing it.

Sometimes materialists try to get away with saying that nothing exists but matter *along with its properties and activities*. If they say this, then they may as well stop calling themselves materialists at all, since neither the properties nor the activities of matter are matter. For example, the motion of matter takes place in space and time, but neither space nor time has mass or takes up space—things have position *in* space, but space just *is* space. Materialists also blithely call forces such as gravity and magnetism "material" phenomena, but a force doesn't have mass or take up space, either. So it seems that even to explain what matter is, we have to suppose the objective and observable reality of things which aren't matter.

And what about our thoughts about matter? They don't have mass or take up space either. "Yes, they do," the materialist may say. "Thoughts are merely something your brain is doing." This materialist opinion has gone through many versions. In the seventeenth century, Thomas Hobbes proposed that thoughts were the motions of tiny, interconnected springs in the brain. Corpuscles of light from a horse strike the eye, the eye recoils, the motion is transmitted to the brain, and there you have it: the thought of a horse. In the nineteenth century, Pierre Jean-Georges Cabanis viewed the process as chemical: "Impressions, upon reaching the brain, make it enter into activity, just as food, by falling into the stomach, excites it to a more abundant secretion of gastric juice, and to the motions which favor their dissolution."[3] Today, materialists view the process as electrical.

But this is hand-waving. Yes, the brain is indispensable to thought, just as vibrations in air are indispensable to speech. But to say that the mechanical, chemical, or electrical events in the brain *just are* thoughts is like saying that the vibrations which convey words *just are* what the words convey. Any electrician can make an instrument which plays a recorded voice saying, "Red!" whenever red light strikes a photoelectric cell, but it would be ridiculous to think that the device has the idea of red.

There are so many things materialism cannot explain, among them meaning, thought, belief, pain, pleasure, the look of a color, the sound of a note, the soul or self, and mental experience in general. Faced with this failure, some materialists desperately resort to what is called "eliminativism." Their idea is that we don't need to explain any of these things—*because they don't exist*! We are not actually having mental experiences, but only *think* we are. We are like that photoelectric cell, except that we are suffering introspective illusions.

This position raises unavoidable questions: If there is an illusion, then what is having it? If *I* am having it, then how can my self be an illusion? If it results from introspection, then what am I looking at in there? Eliminative materialism is so extreme that a consistent eliminativist can't even believe in eliminativism—for beliefs are one of the things he can't believe in.

Chesterton must have anticipated eliminativism when he wrote: "As an explanation of the world, materialism has a sort of insane simplicity. It has just the quality of the madman's argument; we have at once the sense of it covering everything and the sense of it leaving everything out. Contemplate some able and sincere materialist . . . and you will have exactly this unique sensation. He understands everything, and everything does not seem worth understanding."[4]

Just so. In every age there have been scoffers who say that although I may be moved to awe by my beloved's face, the glory I see in it isn't really there. Eliminative materialists outdo ordinary scoffers by a mile. Not only is the glory in my beloved's face an illusion—my awe is an illusion too!

Even if we don't go so far as eliminativism, it seems odd for a materialist to consider his materialism true: For given his premises, how could he know? Even if beliefs really do exist, the materialist must believe that they result solely from material causes. He can't say, "I believe in materialism because it is true," because on his premises, that's not why he does believe in it—he does so only because of things like genes, upbringing, and milieu, material causes with no necessary relation to truth.

For instance, the materialist Richard Dawkins has written that "we are survival machines, robot vehicles blindly programmed to preserve the self-ish molecules known as genes."[5] Yet, inconsistently, he follows up with a call to arms: "Let us understand what our own selfish genes are up to, because we may then at least have the chance to upset their designs, something that no other species has ever aspired to." It is all very stimulating, but of course if we really are "blindly programmed" by our genes, then his call to revolt is worse than futile. One might as well expect a typewriter to revolt against the keys. Perhaps Dawkins is setting his hopes on cultural evolution, for later he suggests that higher-level genetic programs are "open" and do not settle every detail of the way we live. Yet this is hardly a promising gambit either, for his discussion of culture merely exchanges one form of determinism for another. As he sees things, just as our bodies are blindly programmed to preserve the self-replicating molecules called genes, so our cultures are blindly programmed to preserve the self-replicating ideas he calls "memes." Taking him at his word, the "meme" of revolt must be just one more of these replicators. He rails against blind destiny, only because he is blindly programmed to rail against it. This is a strange liberation.[6]

The mistaken view that nothing exists but material bodies probably borrows most of its plausibility from the silliness of the opposite extreme, which is sometimes called "angelism": the view that human beings are entirely non-bodily, that we are pure spirits which happen to use bodies but have no essential relation with them. The classical view, which I defend, is that neither of these opposites is true. We are neither pure bodies, nor pure souls, but unions of body and soul.

Our education makes us suspicious when "souls" are mentioned. To us, the word has the smell of ghost stories. A better way to think of the soul is that it is the *pattern* of the activity in which a living body participates, the formal principle which makes the difference between a lump of dead flesh and an embodied life. When Mr. Smith dies, we don't point to his corpse and say, "Here is Smith, but he has stopped working." Rather we say, "Smith is no longer present. This used to be his body, but now it is only his remains."

In this way of using the word "soul," all living creatures have souls, just in the sense that there are patterns to their embodied lives. But they do not all have souls of the human sort. Our souls are rational; animal souls (for example, cockroach souls) are not. Taking the term in this sense, when people ask "do we have souls?" they are probably not asking whether we have souls, but whether we have *immortal* souls—whether the patterns that characterize our embodied lives can survive our bodies' destruction.

Traditionally, the rationality of human souls has been viewed as suggesting that yes, they may be immortal. I can't settle that matter here, but before closing I want to say something about it—even if for no other reason than the fact that although materialists mock the idea of an eternal soul, few know anything about how the traditional argument works.

Consider the soul—the pattern of the embodied life—of a creature which lives by its senses, say, a beetle. Now a beetle receives sense impressions through its bodily organs without having any rational idea of what they mean. So far as we know, then, everything that happens in beetle life depends entirely on its body. But as we have seen, in the human soul—the pattern of the embodied *rational* life of a human being—certain non-material actions are going on, which cannot be reduced to what its bodily organs are doing. Even the thought, "Over there is another person" goes far beyond what the senses can produce: I don't *smell* personhood. Since some of the actions of the rational soul do not depend on union with its body, perhaps they don't stop when the body stops.

Needless to say, this argument raises further questions, but notice: Even if it is mistaken, it isn't based on sheer faith or biblical revelation. Reason alone gives grounds to think there are more things in heaven and earth than materialists dream.

Lunacy 25

Existence Has No
Meaning Unless We Invent One

ை

It's amazing that a process as amoral and crassly pragmatic as natural selection could design a mental organ that makes us feel as if we're in touch with higher truths. Truly a shameless ploy.*

There is only one really serious philosophical problem and that is suicide.†

In the heyday of existentialism, people like Sartre and Camus lectured the rest of us endlessly about the absurdity of life and the essential meaninglessness of existence. Not many people call themselves "absurdists" anymore, but why not? Have we decided that existence has meaning after all? Not really. It's just that absurdism has dissolved into the culture. So many of us take the idea of meaninglessness for granted that we no longer need to dress it up as an "ism." For someone today to say, "I am an absurdist" would be like saying, "I breathe air" or, "I believe the world is round." No one would have imagined he breathed anything else. No one would have thought he considered the world another shape.

---

*   Robert Wright, *The Moral Animal* (1994).

†   Albert Camus, *Myth of Sisyphus* (1955).

If we no longer chatter about the horror of the abyss, the reason isn't that we no longer find it horrible, but that we avoid thinking about it. Of course, some people still think about it; consider the rising suicide rate. The old, macho absurdists thought they were so brave that they could live without meaning. That was a pose, because nobody can. They merely sought meaning in the *idea* of living bravely. The problem was they hadn't anything to be brave about.

Today, the more common take is, "Meaning is a drag—who needs it? I'm so cool I like life pointless." The TV show *Seinfeld* featured a comedic variation: "I'm so cool that absurdity amuses me. What are you doing for lunch?" This is another pose. Nobody really likes life pointless. Pop absurdists seek meaning in *seeming* to like it pointless, in being cool. The problem is that in a pointless life, being cool is as pointless as everything else.

The highbrow version of pop absurdism is irony. Thomas Nagel's famous essay "The Absurd" concludes, "If *sub specie aeternitatis* there is no reason to believe that anything matters, then that doesn't matter either, and we can approach our absurd lives with irony instead of heroism or despair." But if it's true that nothing matters, then why bother writing an article about it? Why should we care whether we live ironically, heroically, or in despair?[1]

Why do so many of us believe existence to be meaningless anyway? Philosophically, the most common reason for holding this belief lies in materialism, so here we go again. "Man is the result of a purposeless and natural process that did not have him in mind," writes George Gaylord Simpson.[2] William Provine maintains, "No purposive principles exist in nature. . . . No inherent moral or ethical laws exist, nor are there absolute guiding principles for human society. The universe cares nothing for us and we have no ultimate meaning in life."[3] Richard Dawkins opines, "The universe that we observe has precisely the properties we should expect if there is, at bottom, no design, no purpose, no evil and no good, nothing but blind, pitiless indifference."[4] E. O. Wilson and Daniel Dennett write, "Our belief in morality is merely an adaptation put in place to further our reproductive ends . . . an illusion fobbed off on us by our genes to get us to co-operate (so that human genes survive). . . . Furthermore the way our biology enforces its ends is by making us think that there is an objective higher code to which we are all subject."[5] In an earlier work, Wilson pronounces, "Human behavior—like the deepest capacities for emotional response which drive and guide it—is the circuitous technique by which human genetic material has been and will be kept intact. Morality has no other demonstrable ultimate function."[6]

Many people assume such claims to be true simply because those who insist on them are scientists. But even apart from whether other scientists agree with them (far from all do), these writers aren't expressing scientific conclusions, but rather bombast. For example, what does Wilson mean by morality's "demonstrable function"? Why isn't its demonstrable function *showing us what is right*? Wilson's ideology excludes such a possibility, so he simply assumes it out of existence. Since what he *means* by a function is a way to pass genes into the next generation, all he is really saying is, "Morality has no other way to pass genes into the next generation except to pass them into the next generation." The word "demonstrable" adds nothing.

In fact, Wilson hasn't even demonstrated that morality does help pass genes into the next generation. Sometimes it may not. Consider self-sacrifice. If we view genes as the units of natural selection, it's true that sacrificing myself so that my children will live may help pass my genes into their generation, because each of them duplicates half of my genes—including, perhaps, the genes for self-sacrificing behavior. But if this is the only reason for sacrificing myself, then it is hard to see why I should ever sacrifice myself for total strangers. One might try to explain the willingness to sacrifice for strangers as a mere side-effect of genes predisposing us to sacrifice for kin, but on this theory, genes that have such side-effects shouldn't persist in the genome. More finely tuned genes that prompt sacrifice *only* for close relatives—or at least for people we know well—would surely out-compete them.

Or take that idea that morality is "an illusion fobbed off on us by our genes to get us to co-operate . . . making us think that there is an objective higher code to which we are all subject." The premise is that if we think our lives have meaning, we will be more strongly motivated to do those things which enable us to live long enough to pass on our genes. But this reasoning is circular. Belief in meaning would strengthen the motive to do these things only if we possessed a preexisting *need* to believe in meaning—only if we lost interest in living if we didn't believe in it. What adaptive value could there be in this need? Rather than first producing animals who need to believe in meaning, then making them believe in meaning, why didn't natural selection produce animals who don't need to believe in meaning? Anyone not blinded by materialism will conclude not that we seek meaning because it helps smuggle our genes into our descendants, but that *there is meaning*—and we are made with a need to find it.

Unfortunately, there is another, even less creditable motive for the delusion that life if meaningless. The desire to evade knowledge can be almost as strong as the longing to have it. What, then, if life has a meaning, *but we think we may not like it?* Aldous Huxley wrote that for himself and most of his generation,

> the philosophy of meaninglessness was essentially an instrument of liberation. The liberation we desired was simultaneously liberation from a certain political and economic system and liberation from a certain system of morality. We objected to the morality because it interfered with our sexual freedom; we objected to the political and economic system because it was unjust. The supporters of these systems claimed that in some way they embodied the meaning (a Christian meaning, they insisted) of the world. There was one admirably simple method of confuting these people and at the same time justifying ourselves in our political and erotic revolt: we could deny that the world had any meaning whatsoever.[7]

It is almost too obvious to point out that this admirably simple method has lost none of its attractiveness.

But I have been putting something off, for the notion that "Existence has no meaning unless we invent one" has two parts. So far we have discussed only the first—that it has no meaning *in itself.* What about the second—that we can fill in the gap by inventing one? "Things mean whatever you make of them"—isn't that true?

We do "make things" of our lives, for instance by learning trades and raising families; sometimes this is called making meaning. But nothing in life means only what we make of it. I may decide to spend my life taunting children or counting blades of grass, but I can't make life *mean* taunting children or counting blades of grass. Meaning isn't arbitrary even in the details. True, sometimes the underlying meanings of things can be overwritten by contradictory ones, as in a Judas kiss, but it doesn't follow that things have no underlying meanings. The underlying meaning of a slur is malice; of an open-faced smile, good will; of conjugal union, the mutual gift of ourselves.

Yes, we can associate anything with anything. I might associate salami with children because I once ate a salami sandwich while watching children play; I may associate marriage with treachery because a beloved wife was unfaithful. Yet even if "to me" children mean salami or marriage means treachery, the meaning of childhood itself is not salami, and the meaning of marriage itself is not treachery.

If anything at all could mean anything at all, we couldn't even tell each other so. We could communicate nothing. We might as well bubble our lips. We couldn't even engage in interior dialogue, because we couldn't understand ourselves any more than we could anyone else. Even the claim that everything is absurd can be understood only by contrast with the perception that in general, things do mean things. We expect them to; we long for them to; and when we can't perceive their meanings, we despair.

Moreover, even if we disagree about the meaning of life as a whole, we can agree about *what it would mean* to know what life means: It wouldn't mean, say, a nonsense word or the color green, but knowing the truth of the matter.

Truth is not something made up, but discovered. In each piece of meaning we think we've found, we have either got it right or got it wrong. Self-concocted meanings are at best a careless fantasy, and at worst a dangerous deception.

VI

Delusions About God and Religion

It has been said that when human beings stop believing in God they believe in nothing. The truth is much worse: they believe in anything.

—**Malcolm Muggeridge,** *Muggeridge through the Microphone*

Lunacy 26

Religion Doesn't Concern
the Truth About God

∾

Religion ... is the opium of the people.[*]

What's so bad about some opiates, anyway?[†]

One day, while carpooling, the lady with whom I was driving told me that she used to be an atheist, but she wasn't any more. Later during our conversation she praised a certain writer's view of God as a "really neat theology." I thought she meant that the writer's view captured something true about God, or perhaps a reason for believing in God, and I asked her what it was.

She was surprised, taken aback—why would I think she meant that?—and also amused. As she made clear, whether the writer's view contained anything true had nothing to do with her attraction to it. What drew her wasn't that it expressed a striking truth, or even a striking claim about truth, but just that it was striking.

---

*   Karl Marx, *Critique of Hegel's Philosophy of Right* (1843).

†   Stephen T. Asma, *Why We Need Religion* (2018).

Her idea seemed to be that it doesn't matter whether or not a particular religion's claims about God are actually true. Because religion talks about God, God is what it *seems* to be about. But it is *really* about something else. This view pervades our culture.

To some, for example, religion *seems* to be about God, but is really about comfort, or even health. A good religion is a comforting religion, and it doesn't have to be true to be comforting. In pop-therapy language, a good religion takes us to our "happy place." One problem with this view is that no one is comforted by a religion he thinks false. The other is that even if he does think it true, if it isn't his solace is a fraud. Many who don't believe in God pray when endangered. Do they do so because suddenly they believe He exists? More likely, danger makes them realize that they hope He does.

Or perhaps religion *seems* to be about God, but is really about making people good. My gracious host at a religious school to which I had been invited to give a talk about natural law was puzzled by the fact that neither Catholic nor Protestant Christians considered *his* religion Christian. He asked me why. I said I thought the reason was that what his sect taught about the nature of God, the nature of man, and the nature of the relationship between them was opposed to what Christianity claims. His taught that the universe is eternal and that God came into existence in time; Christianity, that God is eternal and created the universe. His, that man is what God once was; Christianity, that man is God's creation. His, that man can be good solely by his own efforts; Christianity, that man is fallen beyond his own ability to repair and requires God's grace.

He answered that, yes, this was so—but that the members of his religion didn't think these beliefs very important, anyway. All that really matters is whether a person is virtuous. What he failed to realize was that "What you believe about God doesn't matter" *is* a belief about God. For it supposes, first, that if there is a God, He doesn't care about our attitude toward Him, but cares only about whether we are virtuous—and, second, that He takes the same view we do of just how splendidly virtuous we are.

Or perhaps religion *seems* to be about God, but is really about making people obedient and compliant citizens. The Establishment Clause of the

U.S. Constitution prohibits setting up an official church, yet we publicly propound what seem to be official religious beliefs. For example, our national motto is "In God We Trust," and the Pledge of Allegiance declares that the nation is "under God," not equal to Him. What about such practices? In 1984, one liberal and one conservative Supreme Court justice argued that they don't violate the Establishment Clause *because they don't actually express belief in God*—they are purely "ceremonial" and have "lost through rote repetition any significant religious content." Oddly, the same two justices held that they are useful for accomplishing "secular" purposes such as solemnizing public occasions, encouraging hope, and "inspiring commitment to meet some national challenge in a manner that simply could not be fully served if government were limited to purely non-religious phrases."[1] I agree that not all public expressions of religious belief violate the Establishment Clause, but the claim that they aren't about God is nonsense. For if these "phrases" really had "lost significant religious content" in the minds of the citizens, wouldn't they have been useless for "inspiring commitment"? Between the lines, these jurists seemed to be saying that the Constitution allows our public officials to express religious beliefs in order to manipulate citizens who believe them, *because the officials themselves don't believe them.* This was an updated version of Plato's Noble Lie.

Then again, perhaps religion *seems* to be about God, but is really about beautiful music and ritual and the feelings they arouse. This was the view of an atheistic colleague who described himself as an "aesthetic Episcopalian," but I wonder. The *Kyrie Eleison,* a chant Episcopalian ritual has borrowed from the Catholic Mass, is moving if you can join in imploring God's mercy. Otherwise it might as well be "The Walrus and the Carpenter," which is clever but hardly moving. "We don't have to believe anything to ask for mercy, do we?" But if you don't believe in God, from whom are you asking it? "We don't have to believe anything just to enjoy the music!" But then why *that* music? For a few generations, people may enjoy Handel's *Messiah* without believing in a Messiah, but the complexity of the music was sustained by beliefs which gave reasons for learning to appreciate it. The next generation may find that the Sex Pistols provide all the melody, rhythm, and timbre they need.

My most revealing encounter with the view that religion isn't really about God but about music, ritual, and feelings took place at a small academic conference in conversation with a man I will call Standish Wanhope. People express themselves so much more preposterously in real life than in fiction that my account may not be believed, but this is what he actually said.

At the first night's group dinner, his conversational opening was unconventionally direct—and a little surreal. "Hello. I'm Standish Wanhope. I'm an atheist." He was like a friendly but aggressive and highly territorial dog, marking the boundaries of his verbal territory every few seconds. The whole conversation was scented with this maneuver. I quickly learned that he claimed to base his ethical philosophy on Darwin, that he had taught at a Catholic college, and that he "had fun ruining all the Catholic kids." It was as though he were boasting of deflowering them.

Our conversation wasn't promising. Picking up on his comment about Darwinism, I asked Standish what he thought of the arguments for intelligent design. He admitted he hadn't read them, but proceeded to lecture me about why they were wrong. To top off the lecture, he recommended what he said was a good critique.

We didn't speak again until the closing dinner. This time, after a few glasses of wine—perhaps more than a few—Standish seemed another person. It was hard to reconcile this Standish with the one who had presented himself the other night. I had to smile; you couldn't dislike him. At least you couldn't dislike this version of him. How the two versions fit together wasn't clear, because this one contradicted everything the one at the opening dinner had insisted upon. He reminded me of Penelope in the *Odyssey*, unraveling every night all she had woven during the day. Reflecting that *in vino veritas,* I was inclined to believe more in this version of Standish than in the other.

With characteristic directness, Standish asked those at our end of the table to tell him our various religious affiliations. We told him. Settling himself in his seat, he exclaimed, "I'm very religious." He told us that during his boyhood he had belonged to one of the old-line Protestant denominations, of which he had fond memories. He had fallen away in his teens, he said, because he couldn't find a reason to believe in God. In a mellow and

170

teacherly voice, declaiming as though he were a stage actor, he said, "I have a deep, rich secular humanism. I'm oh-so-wonderfully satisfied with it."

Since some of those at the table were churchgoers, he asked a little later, "What do you think of the new religious music? To me it's just watered-down Simon and Garfunkel. Give me the fine old traditional hymns any day."

"Where do you hear the new music?" I asked.

"Why, in churches."

"So you visit churches sometimes."

"Yes. But isn't the new music awful?"

"I confess I'd find a steady diet of it difficult. What music do you prefer?"

"You know—the great old songs like 'Rise Up, O Men of God.'"

"Yes, that one sticks to your ribs. What do you like about it?"

"It stirs you up. Makes you want to stand and be counted."

"But for a cause in which you don't believe."

"I told you that I was religious."

"But you don't believe in the religion."

"You aren't understanding me," he said. "Let me tell you something you would never guess. My elderly aunt is a person of deep faith. What a great lady. I still visit her sometimes. It's a moving experience. When I'm with her and she speaks about the Lord, I say, 'I believe.'"

"But you don't believe."

"When I'm with her, I do."

"Then why not when you're not with her?"

"Because I have no rational basis for belief. It's feelings. Feelings aren't knowledge."

"Like your feelings about the grand old Christian hymns."

"Yes. I miss them terribly." He told us that sometimes he sang with a church choir. He had been thinking about joining it, or perhaps he already had—my memory is unclear on that point.

"You would join a church choir without joining the church?"

"Yes," he said. "Just to be able to sing them again."

Just to be able to sing them, I reflected. Just to be able to sing them again. Just to be able to sing them as though they were true.

Standish thought religion isn't really about God, but only about feelings. But one couldn't help but believe that whatever he thought, his feelings were really about God.

Lunacy 27

We Can't Know the Truth About God

❧

What are you to do with a man who puts it forth as a foundation for debate that the human reason is no guide, and who then proceeds to reason through hundreds of pages on that basis?[*]

A writer who says that there are no truths, or that all truth is "merely relative," is asking you not to believe him. So don't.[†]

In the previous chapter I recounted a chunk of conversation with Standish Wanhope. A short time before asking the group what we thought of the new religious music, Standish said he wasn't really an atheist, but an agnostic.

I asked him, "But aren't you an atheist in practice? Although you claim not to know whether God exists, you base your life on the assumption that He doesn't."

He replied, "I don't assume that God exists or that He doesn't exist. Between belief in God and disbelief in God, I'm neutral."

"I understand that you view yourself as neutral. I only suggest that you aren't. Not really."

---

[*]   Hilaire Belloc, *Survivals and New Arrivals* (1929).

[†]   Roger Scruton, *Modern Philosophy* (1994).

"But I am," he insisted. "For all I know Christianity might be true, and for all I know it might be false. I have no information either way."

"The difficulty with that line of reasoning is that it presupposes that Christianity is false," I replied.

"How can not having any information whether Christianity is true presuppose that it isn't true?"

"Because Christianity denies that you have no information bearing on the truth of its claims," I suggested. For if he believed himself ignorant, he must believe at least this Christian claim to be false. And so he couldn't have been neutral about whether or not it was true as a whole.

Unfortunately, this was when he changed the subject and asked our thoughts about the new religious music, so let's consider agnosticism more closely. The agnostic supposes that different religions are equally in the dark about religious truth. Often, he adds that just for this reason, they should all be treated the same. Concerning just how dark the darkness is, different species of agnostics disagree. Rigorists consider it black as the inside of a cave, moderates hold that it is more like the inside of a closet. The former view religious truth as utterly inaccessible to rational inquiry. The latter view it only as relatively resistant to such inquiry—reason may be able to shed a *little* light. But while conceding that people may reasonably disagree about many things, even the moderates view religious truth as more open to reasonable disagreement than the other things about which people make decisions. Presumably these other things include such easy and uncontroversial questions as how to end poverty and war, how to regulate our economies, and how to induce agnostic citizens to start having children again.

Agnosticism closely resembles the religious view called "fideism," for both fideists and agnostics agree that faith and reason are enemies to each other, or at least strangers. The difference is that although fideists and agnostics both say, "Faith and reason are strangers," agnostics add, "I side with reason," while fideists add, "I side with faith." Fideists take the view expressed by Martin Luther when he preached, "Reason is by nature a harmful whore. . . . Ah, but she is so comely and glittering . . . do not follow her beautiful cogitations. Throw dirt in her face and make her ugly."[1]

Although it comes as a surprise to most agnostics, not all religions are fideistic. For example, Catholicism and Calvinism reject the fideistic view. These religions certainly do require faith, holding that certain truths, such as the Trinity and the Incarnation, could not have been discovered just by reasoning; God had to reveal them to us. Yet they require reason, too, believing that the wisdom of the Divine Mind is reflected in the order of Creation. Just for this reason, Creation can be understood by the finite intellect of human beings who are made in His image. Faith and reason, then, are neither strangers nor enemies to each other, but allies. In fact, they complement each other. John Paul II strikingly likened them to the two wings of a bird; both are needed for flight.[2]

Since only some religions are fideistic, the agnostic is placed in the impossible position of defending his policy of viewing all religions as equally in the dark on grounds that fideistic religions are *right* that faith and reason are strangers, and that non-fideistic religions are *wrong*. If some are right and others wrong about the matter, then obviously they are *not* equally in the dark. In fact, the agnostic's plight is even deeper than this. He may say all day that he follows faith and not reason, but how does he know whether reasoning leads to the truth? He cannot demonstrate that it does so *by reasoning*, because that would be circular. He has to base his confidence in the correspondence between reality and reasoning on *faith*—which is just what he supposedly rejects.

Until our own era, when people became uncertain of everything, agnostics didn't say that no truth could be discovered by reasoning. They held only that the truth about *God* can't be discovered that way. It is strange that these supposed champions of reason would deny the power of reason to discover truths about The Most Important Thing. This exception is even stranger when we reflect that to know God is unknowable *would* be to know something about Him.

Indeed, to know God to be unknowable would be to know a great deal about Him. First, one would have to know that even if He exists, He is infinitely remote, because otherwise one could not be so sure that knowledge about Him is so inaccessible. Second, one would have to know that even if

He exists, He is unconcerned with us, because otherwise one would expect Him to have provided us with the means to know about Him. Finally, one would have to know that this hypothetical being is completely unlike the biblical portrayal of Him, because in that portrayal He does care and has already provided the means to know about Him. So, in the end, the so-called agnostic must know quite a number of things about God, just to prop up his claim to be unable to know about Him. The problem is that, on his assumptions, each of these things is impossible to find out.[3]

But what if agnostics are right? What if religious truth really is especially resistant to rational inquiry; what then? Even then it would not follow, as most agnostics think, that different religions should be viewed equally. The consistent agnostic would have to be agnostic on this question, too; he would have to concede that there is no rational way to decide how different religions should be viewed. There might be nonrational ways, such as waiting for a lightning bolt of illumination. Unfortunately, even if he is struck by lightning, he will have no way of knowing whether he should believe what he gets from it. Maybe he is merely suffering an electrical disturbance in the brain.

Perhaps he will say, "Since I haven't yet been struck by lightning and wouldn't know what to make of it if I were, I will proceed on the basis of the *nonreligious* things I know by reasoning. Reason tells me that it's good to get along with people, so I'll just try to treat every religion the same." But that doesn't work either.

In the first place, different religions—for that matter, even different secular ideologies—have different ideas of what it means to "get along." How then can saying, "*This* is what it means to get along, not that!" count as treating them all the same? In the second place, it isn't even *possible* to get along by treating everyone the same. We wouldn't get along better by treating terrorists just like peaceable and law-abiding people. In the third place, if God is the most important thing in all reality, as Christianity claims He is, then reason tells us that fellowship with Him is more important than getting along with everyone. Christ said, "Do not think that I have come to bring peace on earth; I have not come to bring peace, but a sword . . . and a man's foes will be those of his own household."[4] The agnostic might either accept this teaching or reject it, but either way, he is not viewing all religions the same.

Two conclusions follow from all this. First, agnosticism is *theoretically* incoherent. We would have to know an awful lot about God to be sure that we couldn't know anything else about Him. Second, agnosticism is *practically* incoherent. We may say that we don't know whether there is a God, but at every moment we are living either as though there is or as though there isn't.

In fact, the practical dilemma is even deeper than that. For my way of life cannot be neutral about what God is like any more than it can be neutral about whether He exists: I will not be neutral, for instance, as to whether He is a God of love or of hatred. Moreover, to live as though God does *not* exist is effectively to set up something other than God as though it were God. There will always be some Foremost Consideration, some Unconditional Loyalty, some Ultimate Concern. Fill in the blank. The sensual man's "god" is his belly; the greedy man's, wealth; the political man's, his ambition.

The upshot is that agnosticism does not even rise to the level of being mistaken: It is a delusion. The agnostic is not what he thinks he is, because agnosticism is impossible. Willy nilly, he is pursuing some faith—if not this one, then that one. He is merely keeping it a secret from himself.

Better to proceed with eyes open. "Man," wrote Chesterton,

> can be defined as an animal that makes dogmas. . . . When he drops one doctrine after another in a refined skepticism, when he declines to tie himself to a system, when he says that he has outgrown definitions . . . when, in his own imagination, he sits as God, holding no form of creed but contemplating all, then he is by that very process sinking slowly backwards into the vagueness of the vagrant animals and the unconsciousness of the grass.[5]

Lunacy 28

The Truth Is That There Is No God

❧

[O]ur world just seems too ugly to include God in it.[*]

It is not the lie that passeth through the mind, but the lie that sinketh in and settleth in it that doth the hurt.[†]

If by a "proof" you mean an argument so powerful that no one could imagine an objection, then there are no proofs that God is real. The mind cannot be compelled. But in this sense, there are no proofs of anything. Anyone with imagination can doubt anything whatsoever. You can doubt whether kittens meow: "Maybe the ones that meow aren't really kittens." You can doubt that two and two make four: "Maybe my mind is wired so that whenever they make five, I don't notice." But at least we can't doubt our own existence, can we? Because here we are thinking about it! Sure you can doubt it. Prove that every thought requires a thinker.

---

[*]   Steve Dillon, "Why I Don't Think God Exists," *Strange Notions* (no date), https://strangenotions.com/why-i-dont-think-god-exists.

[†]   Francis Bacon, "Of Truth," in *Essays or Counsels, Civil and Moral* (1625).

By now the fallacy becomes obvious. We can doubt anything, but there is a difference between a reason for doubt and a *good* reason for it. We shouldn't believe things because they can't be doubted, but rather because the reasons for believing them are *better* than those for denying them. So it is with belief in God.

Since every conceivable premise can be doubted, we can never come to the end of possible arguments for doubting God's reality. It may be helpful, though, to take a look at five arguments that often come up in conversations about God's existence. Before we consider them, it would be good to remember that mere motives are not the same as arguments. For example, I may be *motivated* to disbelieve in Him because if God is God, then I cannot make myself God. But this would not show that He does not exist.

The first common argument for doubting His reality is that *science has shown there is no God*. Science has done no such thing, unless you define it as a procedure that requires the assumption that there is no God. Harvard biologist Richard Lewontin viewed science that way:

> Our willingness to accept scientific claims that are against common sense is the key to an understanding of the real struggle between science and the supernatural. We take the side of science in spite of the patent absurdity of some of its constructs, in spite of its failure to fulfill many of its extravagant promises of health and life, in spite of the tolerance of the scientific community for unsubstantiated just so stories, because we have a prior commitment, a commitment to materialism. It is not that the methods and institutions of science somehow compel us to accept a material explanation of the phenomenal world but, on the contrary, that we are forced by our a priori adherence to material causes to create an apparatus of investigation and a set of concepts that produce material explanations, no matter how counterintuitive, no matter how mystifying to the uninitiated. Moreover that materialism is absolute, for we cannot allow a divine foot in the door.[1]

There couldn't be a plainer confession. Is science following the evidence wherever it leads? For Lewontin, it requires *not* following it wherever it leads. Evidence is allowed to lead in just one direction. Even absurd explanations must be accepted if they are the only ones that square with materialism.

The second common argument for not believing in God is that *even without assuming His existence, we can still explain everything. Disbelief is thriftier: It makes fewer assumptions.* The elephant in the room is that we can't even explain existence itself unless there is a God. *Oh, yeah? If God created everything, then who created God?* In reply, let's distinguish between what is necessary and what is contingent. Necessary things, if there are any, *have* to exist. By contrast, contingent beings do not have to exist, so if they do, there must be some reason, explanation, or cause for their existence. You and I might never have existed, but we do because our parents conceived us. Now, since the universe itself didn't have to exist, it too needs a cause. Granted, the cause of the universe might be another contingent thing—say, a "multiverse"—but that too would require a cause. There might even be a whole series of things causing things. But the chain must stop somewhere, for unless there is a *first* cause that is not itself caused, nothing is explained at all. Since this needs no other cause, it must exist necessarily. We call this First Thing "God." By the way, this is only one of about twenty arguments for His existence.

The third common argument for not believing in God is that *belief is a crutch—people believe just to comfort themselves.* Some might, but if it comforts someone to believe the sky blue, does it follow that the sky is not blue? Besides, although some people do believe in God for comfort, a good many atheists *disbelieve* in Him for comfort. Philosopher Thomas Nagel offers his own "fear of religion" as evidence: "I want atheism to be true and am made uneasy by the fact that some of the most intelligent and well-informed people I know are religious believers. It isn't just that I don't believe in God and, naturally, hope that I'm right in my belief. It's that I hope there is no God! I don't want there to be a God; I don't want the universe to be like that." He points out that even if natural selection operating by the laws of physics could explain away such things as purpose, meaning, and design, a religious threat might lie in the existence of the laws of physics themselves, or for that matter the existence of anything. The fact that "this seems to be less alarming to most atheists" is "a somewhat ridiculous situation." He concludes that "it is just as irrational to be influenced in one's beliefs by the hope that God does not exist as by the hope that God does exist."[2]

The fourth common argument for not believing in God is closely related to the last: *People believe in Him because they have been brought up to believe. Had they been brought up to believe in Zeus, they would believe in Zeus.* This argument has two fatal defects. First, believing in God is not like believing in Zeus. Zeus was like a Marvel comic-book hero, in that he didn't have to exist; God is the First Cause, He who can't *not* exist. If you disbelieve in God, then existence itself makes no sense. Second, if habit and inertia were the whole story, then we would never see any religious conversions. Actually, conversions are so common that theists and atheists compete in persuading people to change sides. Of course, the motives for changes of heart might all be irrational, but we shouldn't assume that they are without evidence. Is anyone converted just by good arguments? Surely not—but I have never heard of anyone who was converted without his mind having something to say about the matter. With characteristic insight, Pascal reflected that "the heart has its reasons, which reason does not know." Yet the heart and the mind have long talks.[3]

The fifth common reason for not believing in God is that *if He did exist, the world would be a lot different than it is. Consider carnivores: Couldn't He have contrived a world in which the continuation of some creatures never required the death of others?* I am not so sure that the world would be better without lions—but yes, presumably He could have. This argument assumes that God is compelled to create the best of all possible worlds. That is impossible. Since no world could equal His own infinite goodness, for any given world there could be a better one. Divine goodness doesn't require that God create the best possible world, but that in whatever He does create, evil never has the last word—even bad things are turned by Him to some good.

What, even human suffering? Perhaps. We may say that we would willingly trade a world blessed by the courage and patience of martyrs for a world blessed by the absence of their persecutors. Curiously, the martyrs themselves didn't see it this way. We get the word "martyr" from a Greek root meaning "witness," and although the martyrs didn't seek death, they willingly submitted to it so that their witness might glorify God. If this attitude seems inconceivable to us, perhaps we should ask ourselves the reasons.

Assuming that the martyrs were wrong about God, then their death was not beautiful but futile. But the assumption that they were wrong is the very thing we are scrutinizing. The fact that someone who disbelieves it finds their deaths futile does not show that disbelief is true.

I have not suffered anything remotely like martyrdom, but I learned almost nothing during the easy periods of my life. Every insight was hard-won. I learned what a fool I can be through disaster, and how much I loved my father when he was failing and depended on me. I learned what a treasure my wife is when we struggled together through hardship, and the blessing of fatherhood through lost sleep and sacrifice. We tend to detest suffering while enduring it, but long afterward we may be profoundly grateful for it. I would never have chosen to be unemployed, nor would I wish unemployment on anyone else, yet I am grateful to have had the experience. Even looking forward, suffering appears different to me now, when I see the possibility of increasing incapacity ahead of me, than it seemed when I was young. John Donne was right: In some respects, "affliction is a treasure, and scarce any man hath enough of it."

But how could God permit some people to suffer because of others? The natural consequence of my wrongdoing is not only that I damage myself, but that the damage spreads to others. Generations of children suffer for the sins of the fathers. God could have made a world in which no act had consequences, no act had meaning: a world in which, for example, children turned out the same no matter how we raised them. In that case, why bother making parents?

Surely part of the reason was to give finite creatures the astounding privilege of imitating His infinite Fatherhood and participating in governing the universe. By the fact that, for good or ill, just by raising my children I am indirectly helping to raise my children's children, this privilege is not taken away but intensified. If I am a bad father, my descendants may find it more difficult to trust the divine Fatherhood. If I pursue and adore false gods, they are more likely to walk the same false path. So generational consequences are real—but they are the obverse of a blessing: We are placed in a universe in which our actions matter. How would the world be better if we weren't?

Such conversations don't long remain generic. Someone who knows my own faith tradition might object, *That's easy for you to say. Your religion teaches that one day God will cleanse His people's faces of tears, and that He took the burden of human sin on Himself.*

Yes, that is the point. But no, that doesn't make it easy to say. In light of everything else in this life, one must decide whether it is true. Don't be too hasty to say, "No."

Lunacy 29

Judging What Is True or False Is Intolerant

❧

Advertisement for a licensed clinical social worker: "I will never judge anything you say or anything you do. I am insightful, compassionate, and direct."

Woman overheard on an airplane, loudly approving the firing of a coworker for expressing a disapproved opinion: "That's good. He should have been. I can't see why anyone would think that way. I don't. I can't stand people who want to change your opinion."

Suppose we adopt a nonjudgmental attitude about the meaning of marriage. In the old view, marriage requires an exclusive commitment between a man and a woman. The nonjudgmentalist asks, *Who is to say* whether marriage requires exclusivity? A little variety might be fun! *Who is to say* whether marriage requires commitment? We don't know how we'll feel next year! *Who is to say* whether marriage requires a man and a woman? Some men might prefer a harem of women! Notice that "who is to say" is a rhetorical question. To ask "who is to say" is really to insist that *no one is to say,* and that there are no rational principles for answering.

Next we ask, "How dare you discriminate? Since *no one is to say* what marriage is, you aren't allowed to say that it requires a man and a woman." Finally—we discriminate. In the name of nonjudgmentalism, we judge. We say, "You aren't allowed to insist that marriage requires a man and a woman—but *we* are allowed to insist that it doesn't." This eventually becomes the official sexual creed in the law, in the public schools, and in polite society.

So what have we done here? In the name of tolerating all opinions, we have merely replaced one opinion with another. The view which used to define marriage is now defined as bigoted, and the view which used to define transgression against it is now defined as what all right-thinking persons should believe. The same strange inversion takes place in other spheres. Asking *who is to say* which religion is true, we discriminate against belief in God. Asking *who is to say* whether the unborn child is truly a child, we discriminate against those who say he is.

It may seem that only inconsistent nonjudgmentalists would abolish tolerance in the name of tolerance. Surely, consistent ones wouldn't abolish anything. They really would be tolerant. But this is impossible. To be nonjudgmental about everything would require being nonjudgmental about nonjudgmentalism itself. The nonjudgmentalist would have to ask, "*Who is to say* whether tolerance is right?" It's all relative whether we tolerate one religion, six religions, or no religions. It's all relative whether to tolerate rape, murder, or popping gum in theatres.

This is why so-called nonjudgmentalism is never what it seems. It is always a disguise for imposing a moral judgment without having to give reasons for it, just by pretending not to be making one. This doesn't protect against oppression, but encourages it, for *who is to say* what counts as oppressing someone?

But shouldn't we be tolerant? Yes, about some things and in some ways, but proper toleration has nothing to do with not judging. The real reason for tolerating some views we consider mistaken, or some acts we judge wrong, is that the view we judge objectively true *requires* us to do so. This is the classical theory of toleration. Does it sound paradoxical? Consider Hilary of Poitiers, who certainly didn't think all coercion is wrong (we prohibit theft, for example), but did think it wrong to coerce people to worship. In other words, he thought we should tolerate not worshipping. Why? Did he take that view because *who is to say* whether there is a God, whether He has authority, or whether He requires worship? No. In fact, Hilary judged that there is a God, He does have authority, and He does require worship. But as he wrote, "God does not want unwilling worship, nor does He require a forced repentance."[1] In other words, he judged that we can know God to be of such a nature that He abhors the coercion of conscience.

Proper toleration, then, really is a virtue. But it isn't based on suspending judgment—it is based on judging well. We know which bad and false things should be tolerated, because of what we judge good and true.

But now the question *who is to say?* changes into another. For if properly practicing toleration requires knowing something about what is true, then what, in the end, can be known of it?

Quite a bit, and we have been developing the case for this conclusion throughout the book. As we've seen, basic right and wrong are not vague and equivocal, nor are they different for everyone. We never have to do the wrong thing. There is such a thing as good character, and human fulfillment requires it. There is such a thing as the common good, and it cannot be attained without virtue. Marriage is not whatever we want it to be, but has a shape. Neither are manhood and womanhood whatever we want them to be, and the sexes need each other. We share our human nature, though we differ in personality. Human nature is stable and cannot be reshaped at will. We live in the same reality, even though we may have different opinions about it. The world is more than matter, and we are more than bodies in it. Existence has meaning. We can know the truth about God. There is one.

In fact, the most basic principles of right and wrong have been known for thousands of years and substantially acknowledged by almost all human cultures. As we saw much earlier in this book, we possess an excellent summary of it in the Decalogue, the Ten Commandments. Anyone making such a claim may expect fierce protests. *You deceiver, did you think we wouldn't notice that only the Abrahamic religions profess the Decalogue?* But the biblical Decalogue is merely a more perfect expression of that natural law which is dimly known everywhere. People in every place and time recognize that it is good to honor parents, wrong to commit murder, and so on. These are things we *can't not know.*

True, in another way, even what we *can't not know* is controversial. For example, not many people defend murder, but a great many would like to say that abortion is not murder. I say, work it out. Murder is the deliberate taking of innocent human life. Is abortion deliberate? Yes. Does it take a life? Yes. Is the life human? Well, it's not a dog or a porpoise in there. And is the life innocent? Of course it is. The baby didn't force his way in.

Again, even today not many people defend adultery in the narrow sense. On the other hand, the precept has always been understood as a placeholder or metonym for the prohibition of every sort of sexual impurity, including extramarital sex. Every age has its favorite forms of moral carelessness, and casual sex is one of ours. We claim that its prohibition is an irrational taboo, a baseless, hoary scruple. But is it? We have already discussed good reasons to think it isn't.

But if the moral law *is* dimly known everywhere, then why *don't* we live up to it? Our problem is that although the moral law is universal, the desire to escape from it is universal, too.

One of the reasons for confusion is that we don't always feel guilty whenever we violate the moral law. But conscience presses on us even when we don't have guilty feelings, because suppressed moral knowledge has a way of taking revenge. For example, I may exhaust myself trying to avoid thinking about what I have done. Or I may compulsively confess every detail of my wrongdoing *except* that it was wrong. Or I may try to atone for my wrong without repenting it, paying pain after pain, price after price—all but the one price demanded. Or the buried urge to be just may provoke me to endlessly "justify myself," developing elaborate rationales to convince myself that I don't know what I do know, and my wrong wasn't wrong.

Consider cannibals. Their problem isn't that they are ignorant of the wrong of deliberately taking innocent human life. Rather they tell themselves that the fellows in the other tribe aren't human; commonly they even name themselves "the people," implying that those of other tribes are something else. Does that level of self-deception seem ludicrous? Let us not preen ourselves on our superiority to cannibals. Their pretense is no more ludicrous than our pretense that the baby in the womb is not human. For that matter, it is no more ludicrous than most of our pretenses—say, that living together without vows is good practice for living with them. I dare to say that concerning the very basics of morality, no one is truly ignorant, but there is a great deal of denial and self-deception.

The difficulty is that the problem of right and wrong isn't just a problem of knowledge, but a problem of will. The law which is written on the heart of man is everywhere entangled with the evasions and subterfuges of men—and that goes to the heart of this book about delusions, for there is a difference between simple mistakes and motivated irrationality.

For it is not enough to know the truth deep down. I may know it, but prefer not to know it. I may know it, but tell myself that I don't know it. I may know it, but live as though I don't know it. To live in that way is to deny the very truth of my being; it is to be unfree. To be truly free, true to myself, true to the image of God which is my very self, I must want freedom more than whatever snare I may *call* my freedom. I must want to possess truth wholly, and this can happen in only one way. I must be *transmuted* into truth. Everything untrue in me must be burned away.

How much do I want that to happen? It is too little to want it a little. I must want it *completely*, for as our traditions tell us, only the pure in heart receive it. Am I willing to desire that which I do not measure, but which measures me? Can I submit to be ruled and possessed by it? After my last ruse has failed, my last refuge has been penetrated, my last pretense has been dispersed, and I am finally cornered, will I at last yield?

If I cannot yield, am I at least willing to *want* to yield? If I am not willing to want to, am I at least willing to *want* to be willing? Will I at least yield to being helped?

Lunacy 30

The Truth About God Doesn't Matter

∞

I'm not religious. I don't think much about God, except when I am in a pinch and need some special favors. I have no particular reason to think he'll deliver, but I sometimes take a shot anyway. Other than that, I'm just not that interested in God.*

A great many people just aren't interested in whether the truth about God can be known. An online bulletin board contributor asks, "Who cares whether God exists or doesn't exist because in the grand scheme of things, can it really matter what we believe? . . . Look at the bright side. You can now sleep late on Sundays."[1]

This is like asking, "Who cares whether That which is more important than everything else exists? Who cares whether the Source of whatever meaning I myself possess exists?" Considering that our minds are naturally oriented toward knowledge and significance, this needs explanation. I take the writer's reference to the "grand scheme" to mean that even if God exists,

---

*   Steven D. Levitt, "Cut God Some Slack," *Freakonomics* blog (August 2, 2007), https://freakonomics.com/2007/08/cut-god-some-slack.

He is too great to care how we spend our mornings. The writer predicates his indifference to God on God's indifference to him. But then wouldn't he have to *know* that God is indifferent to him? So wouldn't knowing the truth about God matter after all? Besides, it is pretty silly to believe God is too vast to pay attention, because an infinite God would have infinite powers of attention.

Jonathan Rauch, an editor for the *Atlantic,* shares the writer's indifference:

> It came to me recently in a blinding vision that I am an apatheist. Well, "blinding vision" may be an overstatement. "Wine-induced haze" might be more strictly accurate. This was after a couple of glasses of merlot, when someone asked me about my religion. "Atheist," I was about to say, but I stopped myself. "I used to call myself an atheist," I said, "and I still don't believe in God, but the larger truth is that it has been years since I really cared one way or another. I'm"—that was when it hit me—"an . . . apatheist!"[2]

But Rauch's argument is different than the argument of the bulletin-board contributor. He thinks indifference to divine truth is *more virtuous* than caring about it: Haven't we learned from the 9/11 terrorists that people who do care whether God exists mistreat people who think differently? This argument is superficially plausible: After all, if God is a matter of unconditional loyalty, then how can believers *not* persecute nonbelievers? In the prologue to his most recent book, Rauch calls his essay in praise of apatheism "the dumbest thing I ever wrote." Does he mean he was dumb to have no interest in the God question? No, he still thinks people who take an interest in God are terribly dangerous. He only means he was dumb to expect them to disappear. There need to be more virtuous people like him.[3]

From the previous chapter, the naïveté of this view should be clear. Whether caring about the divine truth makes us persecute others will depend on what we think that truth is, won't it? If God, the transcendent source of all being, is the proper object of our unconditional loyalty, then what really follows is that we must adhere to Him in the way that corresponds with His nature. Suppose God, being what He is, detests persecution? Or what if faith, by its nature, is inimical to the forcing of belief? In this case persecution for the sake of God would be rebellion against Him, and persecu-

for the sake of faith would be a crime against it. Even though we may set our faces against Him and seek our own final ruin, not even God will compel us to follow Him. Free will for us was His idea. He likes it.

These are hardly new ideas. As the patristic writer Lactantius explains, "Religion is to be defended, not by putting to death, but by dying; not by cruelty, but by patient endurance; not by guilt, but by good faith. . . . For if you wish to defend religion by bloodshed, and by tortures, and by guilt, it will no longer be defended, but will be polluted and profaned." He says that if someone disinclined to worship is compelled to do so, there is really no worship at all.[4]

We might add that although a person may be motivated to persecute by his devotion to a false view of God, people indifferent to God may also persecute. The Roman emperors were superstitious, but they didn't throw Christians to the lions because they believed fervently in their gods. Emperor worship and the cult of the gods were means of consolidating power and promoting imperial unity. The Christians were threats to both of these goals because they confessed Christ as Lord, not Caesar.

In fact, if the truth about God is anything like what Jews and Christians have thought it to be, then to say merely that a religiously indifferent person *may* persecute is an understatement. Actually the *greater* danger of persecution lies in religious indifference. For if we believe ourselves to be images of the transcendent God, then we have transcendent dignity: We are not just *stuff* to be used and exploited by others, but have inherent rights which no one may violate. The nonjudgmentalist licenses the violation of these rights by asking, "Who is to say whether we have transcendent dignity?" But his cousin, the indifferentist, exposes us to the same danger, because he says, "I don't give a damn whether we have it or not."

An objector may say, "That's not true. I too believe that human beings have transcendent dignity. I just don't give a damn whether or not it comes from our being images of God." But in order to give a damn about our transcendent dignity, wouldn't we have to give a damn about the transcendent source from which it arises? If we don't know from what it arises, then how do we know that we have it? I am not saying that in this case we *can't* believe that we have transcendent dignity, but that in this case we have no idea why we *should* think so, and we may as well not. It's pretty hard to give an account of the transcendent worth of human beings without giving an account of The Transcendent.

Let's be a little more systematic. What would have to be true about God, about man in relation to God, and about the relationship between God and man, for it to be unimportant whether we knew it or not?

Suppose for purposes of argument that the Christian view is true: God exists, He cares about us, we are separated from Him by sin, He has offered a path back to Him, and if we accept it, fellowship with Him is eternal. Then it makes a great deal of difference whether I know this to be true, because if I don't, then I won't accept the offer.

However, someone might argue that if the Christian view is false, then it makes no difference whether I know it to be false. For instance, if reincarnation is true, then I will lead life after life, forever and ever, with no promise of escape from the wheel of becoming. How I fare in each life depends solely on my conduct in the former one. If I behave well, I will be reborn into a better life, and if badly, then into a worse one. It doesn't seem to matter therefore whether I know reincarnation to be true, because what happens to me in the next life will depend solely on my conduct and not my knowledge. Knowing the truth will not help me.

Again, if the materialist has got the facts right, then God does not exist, and this life is the only one there is. Then it doesn't seem to matter whether I know materialism to be true, because those who believe in God will have exactly the same final destinies as those who don't. When they die, they cease to exist. End of story.

These inferences do not follow. Suppose the true story is the reincarnationist one. Then it still matters whether I know, because those who do and those who don't will live differently—at least if they live consistently with their premises. A Christian is not permitted the indolence of fatalism, because he considers himself to have been given the privilege of cooperating in the grace of his redemption. Nor is he permitted callousness toward the sufferings of others, because a part of that privilege is participation in

God's providential care for His creatures. To a consistent reincarnationist, these views must seem misguided. He must regard his situation in this life as an inexorable consequence of his conduct in the previous one—and it is too late to do anything about that. The same belief discourages compassion, for those who are less fortunate must deserve their lot; they are working out the karma from their own previous lives. Of course a Christian may succumb to fatalism, just as a reincarnationist may indulge the natural impulse of compassion. But this happens not because of their respective beliefs, but in spite of them.

Or suppose the materialist view of things is true. In this case, too, it matters whether I know, because it makes a difference to how I live. The materialist and the Christian will approach death differently, for the materialist will either put off death at all costs, or exit life when he no longer enjoys it. Neither course is open to the Christian. The materialist and the Christian will place different valuations on both the pleasures of the body and the possession of material wealth, because the materialist thinks material things are all that exists, and the Christian doesn't. They will take different views of suffering, for the materialist thinks all pain meaningless and futile, while the Christian thinks that although suffering is not good in itself, it can have redemptive value in that it allows him to share in the suffering of the Son of God, who bore suffering and death for him. The Christian will face death with hope, but the materialist will consider hope folly: "Do not go gentle into that good night, / Old age should burn and rave at close of day; / Rage, rage against the dying of the light."[5] There can be such a thing as a materialist martyr, but there can be no such thing as a *consistent* materialist martyr. Any materialist who accepts martyrdom must have caught the scent of some creed other than materialism—Marxism, for example.

Backed into a corner, a nonjudgmentalist might say, "Whatever the truth of God may be, it *just has* to be such that it makes no difference." *Why* does it "just have to"? Perhaps someone can imagine a world in which the truth about God would make no difference. I can't.

If there is no rational basis for indifference, can there be an irrational one? Certainly. From one point of view, God is terrifying. The thing that terrifies us isn't that He might not be good; it's that he might be *too* good. In the sight of an utterly good God, what becomes of flawed beings like ourselves? However, our traditions distinguish between two kinds of fear. The filial fear of God is like the loving awe that a small child has for his father. The servile fear of God is like the fear of a slave who expects to be whipped. If servile fear dominates us, perhaps it isn't so much that we don't care whether we know the truth about Him, but that we would rather not find out.

Since today we live as though there were no God, we habituate ourselves to not believe in Him, even if we don't reason about the matter. What if we did the opposite? Here is an experiment. Have the guts to abandon the pretense of self-ownership. Try living as you would live if you believed God were real. Follow His moral instructions as though you accepted them as His. Admit and repent your wrongdoing as though He were interested. Don't lie about it. Pray every day as though He heard you. Ask Him for grace as though He wanted to give it to you. Worship with other worshippers as though He were worthy to be adored. Keep it up. Day after day, month after month.

See what happens.

Conclusion

❧

*Men, it has been well said, think in herds; it will be seen that they go mad in herds, while they only recover their senses slowly, and one by one.**

We shall be left defending, not only the incredible virtues and sanities of mental life, but something more incredible still, this huge impossible universe which stares us in the face.†

I opened the introduction to this book with the remark that when I speak to groups, I am often asked, "What's happening? Why are we descending into lunacy?" By now it should be clear that I place the *what* before the *why*. We can hardly begin to ask why we are being sucked into lunacy until we understand what we are being sucked into.

And there is something that comes even before that. To understand disease, a physician must first understand health. In the same way, to understand lunacy, we must understand the great patterns of reality from which it deviates.

How far will things go? I don't think any but the most trivial predictions are possible in human affairs, although there is a lot of hoaxing. When a researcher says his model has "predicted" the outcomes of every recent

---

* Charles Mackay, *Extraordinary Popular Delusions and the Madness of Crowds* (1841).

† G. K. Chesterton, *Heretics* (1905).

election, for example, he is really talking about *retrodiction*. Each time the model fails, he tweaks the parameters until it "predicts" what has already happened. Next time it may well fail again.

We are too close to what is happening to see the shape of the future, as an ant is too close to the mountain. Even if the ant were removed to a distance so that he could gain perspective, his eyes are not adapted to the long view. Our situation is only a little better. Besides, we are not billiard balls: Prediction takes account neither of divine providence nor of human freedom. One cannot *predict* a change of heart.

For the same reasons, I don't think it is helpful to conceive grand plans for the rescue of civilization. Yes, of course, when opportunities arise to reform institutional craziness, they should zealously be pursued. But we haven't the perspective to know when we are dealing with root causes of delusion and when we are just trimming the branches. We are too intricately enmeshed in things ourselves. All we really know is that we have passed through waves of delusion before: communism, fascism, now this pandemic of lunacy.

What is clear is that for each person, in each situation, plain duties are close at hand. The main thing is to try to do them, and not be cast down by our failures. Some of us raise children: take care for their souls. Some of us write books: try not to be a fool. Some of us teach students: teach well enough that they learn what you know but aren't ensnared by your mistakes. Some of us run businesses: be honest, and never exploit human weakness for profit. Some of us pursue trades: love excellence. In the meantime, try to think clearly. Never cooperate with lies. Do not be ashamed of the true and the good, but glory in them. Seek the grace of God.

Speaking of God, some say that our lunacies are signs that we are under judgment: "Whom the gods would destroy, they first make mad." I do not have the charism of prophecy, but unlike some of my countrymen, I take such suggestions seriously. It would be eminently foolish to deny that they *might* be true. My country has championed some great causes, but President Ronald Reagan's statement that "America is great because it is good" has always been an overstatement. Yes, we overcame slavery, and that was a great triumph. But now, in our comfort and prosperity, we kill our own babies. If it is really true that God judges the nations, then why should we expect better than what Carthage suffered at the hands of Rome?

It is hardly patriotic to boast that our society is too good to be judged. During the colonial era, teachers thought that love of country demanded the reform of its moral faults, lest God chastise us by allowing us to suffer British tyranny. Thomas Jefferson, who owned slaves, wrote concerning slavery that he trembled for the nation when he considered that God is just and does not sleep. Abraham Lincoln declared in his Second Inaugural Address that the Civil War was a divine judgment on both sides, not just the South, expressing hope that now that slavery had been eradicated the former foes might join to bind their wounds.

Pessimists, quoting Jonathan Swift, will call books like this futile: "Reasoning will never make a man correct an ill opinion, which by reasoning he never acquired."[1] I think Swift would have done better to say that reasoning *alone* will never purge a man of an ill opinion which reasoning did not lead him to adopt. Reason *may* make a difference at certain junctures. The gift of rationality does not mean we can't fall into delusion, but rather that even in their depths our minds can't stop working. Usually they work at digging still deeper into mania, as a paranoid "proves" that everyone is against him. But now and then the defenses slip, and bits of reality, like enemy soldiers, scramble over the battlements. I speak from experience: However deftly we repel reality's soldiers, we cannot quite forget our encounter with them. If the experience happens often enough, we may be sufficiently tempted to peer over the battlements and see what is out there. That is the best an essayist can ask.

How much hope can we actually entertain for the temple to be cleansed of its delusions? Great hope, I think, but nothing is inevitable. We comfort ourselves with the thought that every pendulum eventually swings back: "This, too, shall pass." Yes, everything *does* pass, but not every process is a pendulum, and not every trend reverses itself. One does not expect "the pendulum to swing back" when a deck of cards is collapsing; nor when one is in the path of a tidal wave; nor when a friend is in the last hours of kidney failure.

Of course, because bad ways of living and thinking have natural consequences, the metaphor of the pendulum contains some truth. Eventually
we may catch on: "This isn't going well for us." Unfortunately, one of the
distinctive features of our time is that we have set in place elaborate contriv-
ances for canceling out the natural consequences of things, such as drugs and
contraceptives. It is as though we were trying to grasp the pendulum, to push
it up still higher and prevent it from ever swinging back. But the backstroke
cannot be put off forever. The longer the descent is delayed, the greater will
be its force when it finally comes. It may come with such force as to shatter us.

Like most of us, I would prefer to see our culture renewed and revitalized.
If we are serious about this hope, then we must be brutally honest, because
rejuvenation requires so much intellectual revision, so many changes in our
lives, and so much contrition, that over time, our resistance to doing what has
to be done becomes greater and greater. To justify doing nothing, we adopt
various defensive postures.

Postures like what? One is simple incredulity: *This can't be happening.
Things look okay in my little niche.* Another is shooting the messenger: *If you
think things are as crazy as all that, you must be very disturbed.* Perhaps we
are amused: *All this is just a silly season.* This book began by commenting on
postures like these, but there are more.

Aversion is one: *All the stuff going on is too creepy to pay attention to.* Bore-
dom is another: *Who cares—it's not a real issue like war or the economy.* There
is also obliviousness: *Whatever is happening, it couldn't affect me or my kids.*

Then comes cynicism, the view that *It's only politics as usual,* followed
by mockery, *That's just a conspiracy theory;* by legalism, *All we need to do is
pass a few more laws;* by fear, *I can't speak up because I don't want to lose my
friends or my job;* and by conformity, *I can't bear to think differently than the
people in my milieu.* These postures are followed by complacency, *After all,
people always say the old days were better,* and distraction, *I have plenty of
other more important things to worry about.*

Some people, stupefied, say, *I can't take in the enormity of what is happening.* Others, despairing, mourn that *Everything is inevitable, and I'm on the
wrong side of history.* Still others, perhaps ashamed of themselves, ask, *Who

am I to judge anyone or anything? Hypocrites reassure themselves, *The crazy people are bad, I'm good, and nothing else matters.* People who just want to be left alone dismissively say, *I don't care what happens as long as it isn't shoved in my face.*

And finally, some just capitulate: As Alexander Pope wrote, "Vice is a monster of so frightful mien, / As, to be hated, needs but to be seen, / Yet seen too oft, familiar with her face, / We first endure, then pity, then embrace."[2]

There is a lot of embracing going on.

For how much of our civilizational decline is due to the fact that we like it? Lots. Even people who are worried about it usually like *some* things about it—for instance, I may enjoy sleazy entertainment. Or I may be against abortion in general but want the option open in case my own daughter gets pregnant. Name your poison.

I say these things not to encourage despair, but to encourage us to be more realistic in our practice of hope. We can face lunacy with a cheerful fighting spirit, but a number of hard lessons must be learned. For example, more effort is usually needed to dispel a delusion than to promulgate it. People often respond more to their feelings than to rational argument, and such is the state of our hearts that rational argument may itself provoke fearful feelings. Because various delusions are interconnected, it is probably impossible to target and refute them one at a time. Not only that, but deluded ideas produce disordered behaviors, which reinforce the original ideas. For example, we build relations between the sexes on impossible principles, and then conclude that marriage is impossible and the sexes cannot get along.

For these and other reasons, the idea that our ramifying delusions can simply be "fixed" as one would fix a leaky water pipe is just another managerial illusion. Yet there are things we can do. We can open our eyes. We can counteract the appeal to inappropriate feelings by appealing to appropriate feelings, such as the goodness of family and the exuberant joy of happy marriage. We can meet lunacies not just with counterarguments, but with sounder, more beautiful visions of how things really are. We can cooperate with the restorative tendencies of our nature, and with the grace that supports these restorative tendencies, even short of redemption.

Here is a hard one: We can repent. Those three words are enough to move some people to throw away this book. I hope they won't.

But isn't it good to know that we *can* turn away from lunacy? Nothing requires deluded thinking. We are not in chains. If there is such a thing as God, there is such a thing as grace. Once again, I speak from personal experience.

One step at a time. Even if redeeming a civilization gone awry seems too great a task, maybe you and I can learn to think a bit more clearly. Maybe we can encourage some friends. Maybe our children. Maybe some of our family. I think that would be a lot.

Acknowledgments

❧

Some of the arguments in this book were first tried out in my weekly blog at *The Underground Thomist*. Bits, snippets, and a few paragraphs are also condensed and adapted from other works I have written, as indicated in endnotes, with gratitude to the original publishers.

To the University of Texas, I express appreciation for a research grant that enabled me to spend Fall 2023 finishing another book and writing this one.

I am grateful for the sweetness of my late friend Bill, as well as for the longsuffering of my friend John, who actually is an expert, and the encouragement of my friend Norman, who is not a hothead (John and Norman, see chapters 9 and 16).

This work may be the last that I write. I thank my incomparable wife, Sandra, for putting up with me during its composition, for her never-failing cheer and counsel, and, of course, for loving me when I was deluded, which was no small feat.

Standard Disclaimer

❧

As in all my books, where pronouns are concerned I generally follow the traditional English convention—the one everyone followed before politically motivated linguistic bullying became fashionable—according to which such terms as "he" and "him" were already "inclusive." Except where the context clearly indicated the masculine, they were always used to refer to a person of either sex. Readers who choose differently may write differently; I ask only that they extend the same courtesy to me. In the meantime, since my language includes masculine, feminine, neuter, and inclusive pronouns, any rational being who feels excluded has only him-, her-, or itself to blame.

Endnotes

❧

Introduction

1. This and several subsequent paragraphs are adapted from my op-ed "Some Crazy Ideas Are Deadly Serious," *Wall Street Journal*, March 27, 2023.

2. This is taken seriously: See Sabine Müller, "Body Integrity Identity Disorder (BIID)—Is the Amputation of Healthy Limbs Ethically Justified?" *American Journal of Bioethics* 9, no.1 (January 2009): 36–43, https://pubmed.ncbi.nlm.nih.gov/19132621/. And it is beginning: see Nadia Nadeau, "Successful Treatment of Body Integrity Dysphoria with Amputation: A Case Report," *Clinical Case Reports* (2024): 12:e8720, doi:10.1002/ccr3.8720.

3. To illustrate what goes on: In my own hometown of Austin, Texas, one public school librarian is a BDSM "leatherman"—the letters refer to bondage, discipline, and sado-masochism. An online photograph shows him making a well-known sexual gesture representing "fisting," which is inserting one's fist into another man's rectum. At his initiative, his school invited a drag queen calling himself "Miss Kitty Litter ATX," who had already been reading to children in public libraries, to visit and read to them in the school library. School administrators assured parents that all outside participants in the story hour had been screened, but they concealed the fact that Miss Kitty Litter had received deferred adjudication for homosexual prostitution—in fact, he wrote to the librarian about his status ahead of time and was told not to worry. Unsurprisingly, the stories which were read featured homosexual and transsexual themes. Although the reading was not scheduled to begin until 11:00 a.m., Miss Kitty Litter arrived at 7:25 a.m. and did not leave until shortly before the end of the school day. What he was doing all this time is not known, and it seems he was not required to wear the mandatory school visitor identification badge. Though advocates of "wokeness" deny that this sort of thing is common, the American Library Association confirms that "[m]any libraries across the country have been hosting or participating in Drag Queen Story Hours." Rather than warning parents, the ALA encourages such activities and

207

provides online "resources" to help advocates resist "pushback": See https://www.ala.org/advocacy/libraries-respond-drag-queen-story-hour/. The organization Drag Queen Story Hour has nearly thirty affiliates in twenty states and the District of Columbia. See: https://www.dragstoryhour.org/chaptermap.

4. Thomas Hobbes, "An Answer to a Book Published by Dr. Bramhall" (1682).

5. Alberto Giublini and Francesca Minerva, "After-Birth Abortion—Why Should the Baby Live?" *Medical Ethics* (February 2012), https://jme.bmj.com/content/early/2012/03/01/medethics-2011-100411.full/.

6. *Real Time with Bill Maher*, April 12, 2024.

7. The revenge of conscience is pervasive and multifaceted. I have written about it quite a bit, but my first attempt to address it is the best place to begin: "The Revenge of Conscience," *First Things* 84 (June 1998), https://undergroundthomist.org/sites/default/files/The Revenge of Conscience.pdf.

Lunacy 1

1. Justinian, *Digests*, Title 1, paraphrasing its quotation from Ulpian.

2. Joe Herbert (@herbertmath628), X, July 9, 2020.

3. The associated document is no longer available online, but the workbook, "A Pathway to Equitable Math Instruction Dismantling Racism in Mathematics Instruction," can be found at https://equitablemath.org/wp-content/uploads/sites/2/2020/11/1_STRIDE1.pdf. The mini-course was developed by the San Mateo County Education Office in cooperation with a vast number of private and public partners and collaborators, including the Association of California School Administrators and the education offices of four other California counties, with financial support from the Bill and Melinda Gates Foundation. It was recommended to Oregon teachers by the Oregon Department of Education in a newsletter at https://content.govdelivery.com/accounts/ORED/bulletins/2bfbb9b?fbclid=IwAR3U8iS7fCD-g0NArQh74qlRa5IVFiTXoithZA89kMvmD0DETmzcV9DuQdg.

Lunacy 2

1. "Above all, knowledge of the indefinitely large variety of notions of right and wrong is so far from being incompatible with the idea of natural right that it is the essential condition for the emergence of that idea: realization of the variety of notions of right is the incentive for the quest for natural right." Leo Strauss, *Natural Right and History* (University of Chicago Press, 1953), 10.

2. Clyde Kluckhohn, "Ethical Relativity: *Sic et Non*," *Journal of Philosophy* 52 (1955): 663, in John Ladd, ed., *Ethical Relativism* (University Press of America, 1985), 78–95.

3. John M. Cooper, "The Relations Between Religion and Morality in Primitive Culture," in *Primitive Man* 4 [now *Anthropological Quarterly*] (1931): 36.

4. This fact has been widely misunderstood because of a badly mistranslated passage

in the *Summa theologiae* of Thomas Aquinas. See "The Case of the Germans: Is It Possible Not to Know That Theft Is Wrong?" in J. Budziszewski, *Companion to the Commentary* (Cambridge University Press, 2014), 155–59, available at no cost at https://www.cambridge.org/files/3614/2469/5786/9781107029392_-_Companion_to_the_Commentary.pdf.

5. Franz Stangl, former commandant of the Treblinka death camp, quoted in Gitta Sereny, *Into That Darkness: An Examination of Conscience* (Vintage Books, 1983), 101.

6. "Ain't No Wrong," song by Jane's Addiction. The band won an MTV award in 1991 and a Webby award in 2012, and it has been nominated for various other awards, including Grammys.

7. Debbie Hampton, "My Reality Is Not Your Reality," *Your Best Brain Possible* (September 8, 2014), https://thebestbrainpossible.com/my-reality-is-not-your-reality-2/.

8. David T. Lykken, *The Antisocial Personality* (Lawrence Erlbaum Associates, 1995), 28.

Lunacy 3

1. Donald Miller, *Masters of the Air: America's Bomber Boys Who Fought the Air War Against Nazi Germany* (Simon & Schuster, 2007), 431.

2. John Harris, "The Survival Lottery," in Peter Singer, ed., *Applied Ethics* (Oxford University Press, 1986).

3. As recommended here: "The only remedy to racist discrimination is antiracist discrimination. The only remedy to past discrimination is present discrimination. The only remedy to present discrimination is future discrimination." Ibram X. Kendi, *How to Be an Antiracist* (One World, 2019), 19.

4. Flannery O'Connor, *A Memoir of Mary Ann* (Farrar, Straus and Cudahy, 1961).

5. John Harris's profile at the Oxford Uehiro Centre for Practical Ethics declares, "Recently, perhaps the most famous figure in contemporary philosophy, the editor of the influential *Review of Applied Ethics*, Isabel Dalhousie, in a rare appraisal of a living philosopher, characterized Harris as 'a kind man and a very subtle philosopher.'" See https://www.practicalethics.ox.ac.uk/people/professor-john-harris.

Lunacy 4

1. William L. Riordon, *Plunkitt of Tammany Hall* (A. A. Knopf, 1948: repr. Signet, 2015), 1.

2. John M. Darley and C. Daniel Batson, "From Jerusalem to Jericho: A study of Situational and Dispositional Variables in Helping Behavior." *Journal of Personality and Social Psychology* 27, no. 1 (1973): 100–108.

3. For example, Gilbert Harman, "No Character or Personality," *Business Ethics Quarterly* 13, no. 1 (2003): 87–94.

Lunacy 5

1. Alexander Pope, *Essay on Man*, Epistle 4 (1733–34).
2. Martin E. P. Seligman, in Corey L. M. Keyes and Jonathan Haidt, eds., *Flourishing: Psychology and the Life Well-Lived* (American Psychological Association, 2003), xii; cf. xvi.
3. Mortimer J. Adler, *The Time of Our Lives: The Ethics of Common Sense* (Fordham University Press, 1970).
4. Jeremy E. Sherma, "Virtue-Maxing: A Stupifying, Universally-Popular Moral Myth," *Psychology Today* blog (May 31, 2021), https://www.psychologytoday.com/us/blog/ambigamy/202105/virtue-maxing-stupifying-universally-popular-moral-myth.

Lunacy 6

1. The origin of this aphorism is disputed, but it has been attributed to various totalitarians.
2. The rest of this chapter adapts paragraphs, with gratitude to the publisher, from my *Public Discourse* article "Between Man and Man: Friendship, Law, and the Common Good" (May 15, 2021), https://www.thepublicdiscourse.com/2021/05/75748/, which was in turn based on my presentation to the Common Good Project, College of Law, Oxford University, "The Flavors of the Common Good" (March 2, 2021), https://www.youtube.com/watch?v=XZ5AlD0ofDc/.
3. Thomas Aquinas, *Summa theologiae,* II-II, Q. 30, Art. 2.

Lunacy 7

1. Although I am attributing to Witherspoon the *idea* that every nation has the government it deserves, it fell to the French thinker Joseph de Maistre, in letters of 1811 and 1816, to reduce this idea to a maxim.
2. John Witherspoon, "The Dominion of Providence Over the Passions of Men" (1776), delivered shortly before his election to the Continental Congress.
3. *Federalist,* no. 51, by Alexander Hamilton (possibly James Madison).
4. David Hume, *Essays, Moral, Political, and Literary* (1742), Part 1, Essay 3.
5. James Madison at Virginia Ratifying Convention, June 20, 1788.
6. See the end of the chapter on Lunacy 10.
7. *Federalist,* no. 10, by James Madison.

Lunacy 8

1. Pew Research Center, "Values and Expectations of Government" (June 6, 2022), https://www.pewresearch.org/politics/2022/06/06/values-and-expectations-of-government/.
2. See Marvin Olasky, *The Tragedy of American Compassion* (Regnery Publishing, 1992).

Lunacy 9

1. Anthony Fauci on *Face the Nation*, November 28, 2021.
2. https://gbdeclaration.org
3. See the committee's press release at: https://oversight.house.gov/release/wenstrup-releases-statement-following-dr-faucis-two-day-testimony/.
4. Nicholas Wade, "Where Did COVID Come From?" *Wall Street Journal* (February 28, 2024), https://www.wsj.com/articles/where-did-covid-come-from-new-evidence-lab-leak-hypothesis-78be1c39/. For a much more detailed discussion, see Wade's earlier article, "The Origin of COVID: Did People or Nature Open Pandora's Box at Wuhan?" *Bulletin of the Atomic Scientists* (May 5, 2021), https://thebulletin.org/2021/05/the-origin-of-covid-did-people-or-nature-open-pandoras-box-at-wuhan/.
5. See Michael J. Behe, *Darwin's Black Box: The Biochemical Challenge to Evolution,* 2d ed. (Free Press, 2006).
6. See Patrick T. Brown, "I Left Out the Full Truth to Get My Climate Change Paper Published," *The Free Press* (September 5, 2023), https://www.thefp.com/p/i-overhyped-climate-change-to-get-published/.
7. John P. S. Ioannis, "Why Most Published Research Findings Are False," *PLOS Medicine* 2, no. 8 (August 2005), available at https://journals.plos.org/plosmedicine/article?id=10.1371/journal.pmed.0020124/.

Lunacy 10

1. For a graphical summary, see https://www.rmgresearch.com/wp-content/uploads/2024/01/Elite-One-Percent.pdf.
2. Paul Johnson, *Intellectuals: From Marx and Tolstoy to Sartre and Chomsky* (Harper and Row, 1988), 342.
3. "The Supreme Court: A Seat for Mediocrity?" *Time* (March 30, 1970), https://content.time.com/time/subscriber/article/0,33009,942208,00.htm/l.
4. William F. Buckley Jr., *Rumbles Left and Right: A Book about Troublesome People and Ideas* (G. P. Putnam's Sons, 1963), 134.

Lunacy 11

1. Data from https://www.cdc.gov/nchs/data/nvsr/nvsr48/nvs48_16.pdf and https://www.statista.com/statistics/276025/us-percentage-of-births-to-unmarried-women/.
2. Data from https://www.cdc.gov/nchhstp/newsroom/fact-sheets/std/std-us-2020.html.
3. Quoted in Maggie Gallagher, "Second Thoughts," review of *Last Night in Paradise: Sex and Morals at the Century's End,* by Katie Roiphe, *National Review* (March 24, 1997), 52.

4. Mary Harrington, "Smartphones Have Turbocharged the Danger of Porn," *Wall Street Journal* (October 13, 2023), https://www.wsj.com/tech/smartphones-have-turbocharged-the-danger-of-porn-a701eeaf/.

5. Nona Willis Aronowitz, "I Still Believe in the Power of Sexual Freedom," *New York Times* (August 16, 2022), https://www.nytimes.com/2022/08/16/opinion/sex-women-feminism-rules.html.

6. Anna Louie Sussman, "Why Aren't More People Marrying? Ask Women What Dating Is Like," *New York Times* (November 11, 2024), https://www.nytimes.com/2023/11/11/opinion/marriage-women-men-dating.html.

7. Jennifer Moses, "Why Do We Let Them Dress Like That?" *Wall Street Journal*, March 19, 2011.

8. Meghan Dillon, "Virgin Shaming Is the New Slut Shaming, and It Needs to Stop," *Evie* (April 22, 2020), https://www.eviemagazine.com/post/virgin-shaming-is-the-new-slut-shaming-and-it-needs-to-stop/.

Lunacy 12

1. "Why Can't a Woman Be More Like a Man?" from *My Fair Lady* (music by Frederick Loewe, lyrics by Alan Jay Lerner).

2. "Women in Science Are Doing All Right," *Wall Street Journal* (April 30, 2023), https://www.wsj.com/articles/the-female-scientists-are-all-right-women-engineering-wage-gap-sexism-discrimination-b186f9d9?mod=article_inline.

3. Letter to the editor of the *Wall Street Journal*, published as, "Women in Science Aren't Doing 'All Right,'" *Wall Street Journal* (May 3, 2023), https://www.wsj.com/articles/women-in-science-sexism-academia-f3cc621d/.

4. Rosemary L. Hopcroft, "More Babies for the Rich? The Relationship between Status and Children Is Changing." Institute for Family Studies (blog), March 18, 2024, https://ifstudies.org/blog/more-babies-for-the-rich-the-relationship-between-status-and-children-is-changing/.

5. Alia E. Dastagir, "Marsha Blackburn Asked Ketanji Brown Jackson to Define 'Woman.' Science Says There's No Simple Answer." *USA Today* (March 22, 2022), https://www.usatoday.com/story/life/health-wellness/2022/03/24/marsha-blackburn-asked-ketanji-jackson-define-woman-science/7152439001/.

6. The rest of this chapter is adapted, with gratitude to the publisher, from a much longer discussion in my book *On the Meaning of Sex* (ISI Books, 2014).

7. Interview with Alice von Hildebrand, Zenit news service (November 23, 2003), http://www.zenit.org/article-8793?l=english.

8. Edith Stein, *Essays on Woman,* 2d ed., trans. Freda Mary Oben, constituting Volume 2 of Lucy Gelber and Romaeus Leuven, *Collected Works of Edith Stein* (ICS Publications, 1996).

Lunacy 13

1. Several paragraphs of this chapter have been adapted, with gratitude to the publisher, from a much longer discussion in my book *On the Meaning of Sex* (ISI Books, 2014).
2. Sara McLanahan and Gary Sandefur, *Growing Up with a Single Parent: What Hurts, What Helps* (Harvard University Press, 1994), 38.
3. Joseph Henrich, Robert Boyd, and Peter J. Richerson, "The Puzzle of Monogamous Marriage," *Philosophical Transactions of the Royal Society B* 367 (2012): 657–69. By "democratic," they mean, of course, republican.
4. Kim Parker and Rachel Minkin, "Views of Divorce and Open Marriages," Pew Research Center (September 14, 2023), https://www.pewresearch.org/social-trends/2023/09/14/views-of-divorce-and-open-marriages/.
5. "Kira," quoted in Ashley Rockman, "A Glimpse into the Lives of Couples with Open Marriages," *Huffington Post* (November 18, 2014), https://www.huffpost.com/entry/the-new-i-do-excerpt_n_6111242/.
6. See for example W. Bradford Wilcox, "The Evolution of Divorce," *National Affairs* 38 (Winter 2019), https://www.nationalaffairs.com/publications/detail/the-evolution-of-divorce/.
7. Interview with Wilcox at https://live.washingtonpost.com/onlove-pitfalls-of-cohabitation.html.
8. See Brad Wilcox and Lyman Stone, "Too Risky to Wed in Your 20s? Not If You Avoid Cohabiting First," *Wall Street Journal* (February 5, 2022), https://www.wsj.com/articles/too-risky-to-wed-in-your-20s-not-if-you-avoid-cohabiting-first-11644037261?page=1.
9. This is even more likely in view of the fact that many who cohabit before marriage have done so with more than one partner; they already have experience breaking up.

Lunacy 14

1. Paraphrasing Alan Feingold, "Gender Differences in Personality: A Meta-Analysis," *Psychological Bulletin* 116 no. 3 (1994): 429–56, and Paul T. Costa Jr., Antonio Terracciano, and Robert R. McCrae, "Gender Differences in Personality Traits Across Cultures: Robust and Surprising Findings," *Journal of Personality and Social Psychology* 81 no. 2 (2001): 322–31. The research of Costa, et al., broadens Feingold's conclusions about sex differences to a wider range of cultures and personality traits.
2. This paragraph, along with parts of several subsequent paragraphs, are adapted, with gratitude to the publisher, from a much longer discussion in my book *On the Meaning of Sex* (ISI Books 2014).
3. Paraphrasing Larry Cahill, "Why Sex Matters for Neuroscience," *Nature Reviews: Neuroscience* 7 (2006), 477–84, Larry Cahill, "His Brain, Her Brain," *Scientific American* 292 no. 5 (2005): 40–47, and Doreen Kimura, "Sex Differences in the Brain," *Scientific American* 267 no. 3 (1992): 119–25.

4. David P. Schmitt, "The Truth About Sex Differences," *Psychology Today* (November 7, 2017), https://www.psychologytoday.com/us/articles/201711/the-truth-about-sex-differences/.

5. Curtis Crane, "Ask Me Anything: Non-Binary Surgery," posted July 1, 2020, by Crane Center, YouTube, https://www.youtube.com/watch?v=_99AsK7uBDA/.

6. Video clip of Laura A. Jacobs, posted by Genspect (@genspect), X, March 20, 2024, https://twitter.com/genspect/status/1770637625143050571/.

7. The number has been widely reported as ninety-seven, but that includes "I don't use labels" and "declined." See the "Documents" section at https://www.giftincome.org/apply/.

8. Definition from https://gender.fandom.com/wiki/Xenogender?wikia-footer-wiki-rec=true/.

9. Objectùm-Sexuality Internationale, http://www.objectum-sexuality.org. See also Steven Tucker, "On Valentine's Day, How About Celebrating the New Campaign for Marriage to Inanimate Objects?" Mercatornet.org (February 12, 2024).

10. Kelly-Ann Mills and Jasmine Kazlauskas, "Woman, 24, Who Is Sexually Attracted to Objects Marries 'Love of Her Life' Briefcase," *Mirror* (December 14, 2020), https://www.mirror.co.uk/news/world-news/woman-24-who-sexually-attracted-23164716/.

11. Allyn Walker, quoted in Ian Oxnevad, "Professor's Redefinition of Pedophilia Could Help Offenders Demand Rights (January 1, 2022), https://nypost.com/2022/01/01/professors-redefinition-of-pedophilia-could-help-offenders-demand-rights.

12. https://en.wikipedia.org/wiki/Fictosexuality, accessed February 15, 2024.

13. Susan K. Livio, "Is Your Baby Straight or Gay? N.J. Hospitals Hand Out Controversial Forms to New Moms," NJ.com (March 10, 2025), https://www.nj.com/politics/2025/03/mom-shocked-and-disgusted-by-nj-hospital-form-asking-babys-sexual-orientation.html.

14. Katie J. M. Baker, "When Students Change Gender Identity, and Parents Don't Know," *New York Times* (January 22, 2023), https://www.nytimes.com/2023/01/22/us/gender-identity-students-parents.html.

15. Dan Springer, "Washington Bill Will Allow Runaway Kids to Get Sex Change Surgeries" (April 25, 2023), https://www.foxnews.com/politics/laws-protecting-gender-surgeries-children-advance-washington-oregon-over-republican-objections/.

16. Walt Heyer, "Transgender Regret Is Real Even If the Media Tell You Otherwise," *Federalist* (August 19, 2015), https://thefederalist.com/2015/08/19/transgender-regret-is-real-even-if-the-media-tell-you-otherwise/.

17. Cecilia Dhejne, Paul Lichtenstein, Marcus Boman, Anna L. V. Johansson, Niklas Långström, and Mikael Landén, "Long-Term Follow-Up of Transsexual Persons Undergoing Sex Reassignment Surgery: Cohort Study in Sweden." *PLOS ONE* 6 vol. 2 (February 22, 2011), https://doi.org/10.1371/journal.pone.0016885.

18. Sami-Mati Ruuska, Katinka Tuisku, Timo Holttinen, and Riittakerttu Kaltiala, "All-Cause and Suicide Mortalities Among Adolescents and Young Adults Who

Contracted Specialised Gender Identity Services in Finland 1996–2019: A Register Study," *BMJ Mental Health* 27 (2025): 5.

19. U.S. Department of Health and Human Services, "Treatment for Pediatric Gender Dysphoria: Review of Evidence and Best Practices" (May 1, 2025), https://opa.hhs. gov/sites/default/files/2025-05/gender-dysphoria-report.pdf.

20. Walt Heyer, "Hormones, Surgery, Regret: I Was a Transgender Woman for Eight Years," *USA Today* (February 11, 2019), https://www.usatoday.com/story/opinion/ voices/2019/02/11/transgender-debate-transitioning-sex-gender-column/1894076002/

21. One bestselling book was "cancelled," or banned, by Amazon just because it meticulously documented some unwelcome facts. The book was Ryan T. Anderson's *When Harry Became Sally: Responding to the Transgender Moment* (Encounter Books, 2019).

22. Jamie Shupe, "I Was America's First 'Nonbinary' Person. It Was All a Sham," (March 12, 2019), https://www.mercatornet.com/conjugality/view/i-was-americas-first-nonbinary-person.-it-was-all-a-sham/22275.

23. Henry Carnell and Madison Pauly, "'An Anti-Trans Fever Dream': HHS Publishes Attack on Gender-Affirming Youth Care," *Mother Jones* (May 1, 2025), https://www. motherjones.com/politics/2025/05/hhs-trans-youth-gender-care-report.

Lunacy 15

1. Genesis 1:23, 2:12, emphasis added.

2. "I Don't Need a Woman," song by R. L. Boyce.

3. "No Man," song by Nina Storey.

4. Tracy Ann, "Women Don't Need Men to Complete Them, This Ain't Fill in the Blanks," *iDiva* (February 26, 2019), https://www.idiva.com/relationships-love/ relationships/solid-reasons-why-women-dont-need-men-to-complete-them/17079455/.

Lunacy 16

1. Marcus Tullius Cicero, *De officiis* (On Duties), trans. Walter Miller (Harvard University Press, 1913), Book 1, Section 107.

2. "Genetics of Alcohol Use Disorder," National Institute of Alcohol Abuse and Alcoholism, National Institutes of Health, https://www.niaaa.nih.gov/alcohols-effects-health/alcohol-use-disorder/genetics-alcohol-use-disorder/.

3. Paul Sullins, "'Born That Way' No More: The New Science of Sexual Orientation," *Public Discourse* (September 30, 2019), https://www.thepublicdiscourse.com/2019/ 09/57342/; Andreana Ganna, et al., "Large-Scale GWAS Reveals Insights into the Genetic Architecture of Same-Sex Sexual Behavior," *Science* 355 no. 6456 (August 30, 2019), https://www.science.org/doi/10.1126/science.aat7693/.

4. Anna Silman, "A History of Woody Allen and Soon-Yi Previn Describing Their Relationship, from 'The Heart Wants What It Wants' to 'I Was Paternal,'" *Salon* (July

30, 2015), https://www.salon.com/2015/07/30/a_history_of_woody_allen_and_soon_
yi_previn_describing_their_relationship_from_the_heart_wants_what_it_wants_
to_i_was_paternal/.

Lunacy 17

1. Psalm 139:14 (KJV).
2. Kara Babcock, review of *Machine Man*, by Max Barry, Goodreads (August 7, 2011), https://www.goodreads.com/book/show/6634696-machine-man/.
3. "The Bad Touch," song by the Bloodhound Gang.
4. https://www.reddit.com/r/awakened/comments/pxuexr/humans_are_just_animals/?rdt=3290, punctuation corrected.
5. G. K. Chesterton, *Orthodoxy* (The Bodley Head, 1908), Chapter 9.
6. https://www.quora.com/I-hate-how-humans-are-so-arrogant-The-Human-race-say-they-are-superior-than-other-animals-Animals-dont-destroy-the-environment-animals-dont-have-wars-and-they-dont-waste-their-time-taking-selfies-Why-do-I-think-this.
7. Addis Hunde Bedada, "CAHFS Weekly Update: The Worst Desert Locust Crisis" (May 28, 2020), https://cahfs.umn.edu/news/cahfs-weekly-update-worst-desert-locust-crisis/.
8. Jane Goodall, *Through a Window: My Thirty Years with the Chimpanzees of Gombe* (Houghton Mifflin Harcourt, 1990; repr., Mariner Books, 2010), 126.

Lunacy 18

1. Timothy P. Carney, quoted in an interview with Katrina Trinko, "What Our Baby Bust Says About Modern America," *The Daily Signal* (March 26, 2024), https://www.dailysignal.com/2024/03/26/what-our-baby-bust-says-about-modern-america/.
2. "Most People Are Good," song by Luke Bryan.
3. "People Are Good," song by Depeche Mode.
4. *The Book of Mencius*, Book 6, Part 1, in Wing-Tsit Chan, trans., *A Source Book in Chinese Philosophy* (Princeton University Press, 1972), 51, 54.
5. "The Nature of Man Is Evil," *The Hsün Tzu*, 128–32.
6. John Calvin, *Institutes of the Christian Religion*, Book 4, Chapter 15, trans. Henry Beveridge (1845; orig. 1536), https://ccel.org/ccel/calvin/institutes/institutes.i.html.
7. Calvin, *Institutes*, Book 2, Chapter 2.
8. Calvin, *Institutes*, Book 1, Chapter 14.
9. Jean-Jacques Rousseau, *Discourse on the Origin of Inequality Among Men* (1754).
10. Gareth Cook, "The Moral Life of Babies," *Scientific American* (November 12, 2013), https://www.scientificamerican.com/article/the-moral-life-of-babies/.
11. G. K. Chesterton, *Orthodoxy* (The Bodley Head, 1905), Chapter 2.

Lunacy 19

1. Alexander Solzhenitsyn, *The Gulag Archipelago* (Harper and Row, 1973), 562.
2. José Ortega y Gasset, "Man Has No Nature," from *History as a System*, in Walter Kaufmann, ed., *Existentialism from Dostoevsky to Sartre*, rev. ed. (New American Library, 1975), 157.
3. Jean-Paul Sartre, *Existentialism and Human Emotions* (Kensington Publishing, 1987), 15.

Lunacy 20

1. Mihail C. Roco and William Sims Bainbridge, eds., "Converging Technologies for Improving Human Performance: Nanotechnology, Biotechnology, Information Technology and Cognitive Science" (National Science Foundation and U.S. Department of Commerce, June 2002), https://www.academia.edu/26151799/Converging_Technologies_for_Improving_Human_Performance/.
2. Gary Marcus and Christof Koch, "The Plug-and-Play Brain," *Wall Street Journal* (March 15, 2014); online as "The Future of Brain Implants," https://www.wsj.com/articles/SB10001424052702304914904579435592981780528.
3. This paragraph and the next two are adapted, with gratitude to the publisher, from my *First Things* essay "The Uses of Death" (August 2023).

Lunacy 21

1. So-called fuzzy logic is multivalued logic. He actually meant paraconsistent logic. This anecdote, and several subsequent paragraphs, are adapted, with gratitude to the publisher, from my book *Commentary on Thomas Aquinas's Treatise on the Doctrine of God* (Cambridge University Press, 2024).
2. Joe Herbert (@herbertmath628), X, July 9, 2020.
3. Antonio Spadaro (@spadaroantonio), X, January 5, 2017.

Lunacy 22

1. Debbie Hampton, "My Reality Is Not Your Reality," *Your Best Brain Possible* (September 8, 2014), https://thebestbrainpossible.com/my-reality-is-not-your-reality-2/.
2. Anil K. Seth, "The Neuroscience of Reality," *Scientific American* (September 1, 2019), https://www.scientificamerican.com/article/the-neuroscience-of-reality/.
3. Erwin Schrödinger, "Die Gegenwärtige Situation in der Quantenmechanik," *Naturwissenschaften* 23 no. 48 (November 1935): 807–12. Translated by John D. Trimmerin as "The Present Situation in Quantum Mechanics: A Translation of Schrödinger's 'Cat Paradox' Paper," in *Proceedings of the American Philosophical Society* 125 no. 5 (1980): 323–38.

Lunacy 23

1. https://www.youtube.com/watch?v=xfO1veFs6Ho.
2. Post by helplessdelta to the topic thread "Generational labels are arbitrary and based on nothing," Reddit (c. 2019), https://www.reddit.com/r/unpopularopinion/comments/f20r26/generational_labels_are_arbitrary_and_based_on/?rdt=58078/.
3. G. K. Chesterton, "The Suicide of Thought," in *Orthodoxy* (The Bodley Head, 1908).

Lunacy 24

1. "Material Girl," song by Madonna.
2. "Matter," *Encyclopedia Britannica* (accessed October 2, 2023), https://www.britannica.com/science/matter.
3. Pierre Jean-Georges Cabanis, *Rapports du Physique et du Moral de l'Homme* [Relations Between the Physical and Moral in Man] (1802).
4. G. K. Chesterton, *Orthodoxy* (The Bodley Head, 1908), chapter 2.
5. Richard Dawkins, *The Selfish Gene* (Oxford University Press, 1989), 3.
6. This paragraph is adapted from a much longer discussion in my book *The Line Through the Heart: Natural Law as Fact, Theory, and Sign of Contradiction* (ISI Books, 2011).

Lunacy 25

1. Thomas Nagel, "The Absurd," *Journal of Philosophy* 68 no. 20 (October 1971): 716–27.
2. George Gaylord Simpson, *The Meaning of Evolution*, rev. ed. (Yale University Press, 1967), 344–45.
3. William Provine, "Scientists, Face it! Science and Religion Are Incompatible," *The Scientist* (September 5, 1988), 10–11.
4. Richard Dawkins, *River Out of Eden* (HarperCollins, 1995), 132–33.
5. Michael Ruse and E. O. Wilson, "The Evolution of Ethics," *New Scientist* 108 no. 1478 (October 17, 1985): 51–52.
6. Edward O. Wilson, *On Human Nature* (Harvard University Press, 1978), 176.
7. Aldous Huxley, *Ends and Means: An Enquiry into the Nature of Ideals and into the Methods Employed for Their Realization* (Chatto & Windus, 1937; repr. Routledge, 2017), 316.

Lunacy 26

1. *Lynch v. Donnelly*, 465 U.S. 668 (1984), dissenting opinion of Justice William J. Brennan and concurring opinion of Justice Sandra Day O'Connor.

Lunacy 27

1. Martin Luther, "Last Sermon in Wittenberg" (1546), in J. B. Doberstein and H. T. Lehmann, eds., *Luther's Works*, vol. 51 (Muhlenberg Press, 1959), 376.

2. "Faith and reason are like two wings on which the human spirit rises to the contemplation of truth; and God has placed in the human heart a desire to know the truth—in a word, to know himself—so that, by knowing and loving God, men and women may also come to the fullness of truth about themselves." John Paul II, *Fides et Ratio* (encyclical letter, 1998), preface.

3. This and several subsequent paragraphs are adapted, with gratitude to the publisher, from a longer discussion in my chapter "Natural Law, Democracy, and Shari'a," in Rex Ahdar and Nicholas Aroney, eds., *Shari'a in the West* (Oxford University Press, 2011).

4. Matthew 10:34–36 (RSV-CE).

5. G. K. Chesterton, *Heretics* (John Lane Co., 1905), 286.

Lunacy 28

1. Richard Lewontin, "Billions and Billions of Demons," *New York Review of Books* 44 no. 1 (January 9, 1997): 28–32.

2. Thomas Nagel, *The Last Word* (Oxford University Press, 1996), 130–31.

3. Blaise Pascal, *Pensées*, trans. W. F. Trotter (1670), section 277.

Lunacy 29

1. Hilary, *To Constantius*, quoted in John Emerich Edward Dalberg-Acton, "Political Thoughts on the Church," in J. Rufus Fears, ed., *Selected Writings of Lord Acton*, vol. 3 (Liberty Classics, 1988), 24.

Lunacy 30

1. Post by qazwart to the topic thread "Is There a God?" (December 11, 2011), *Straight Dope*, https://boards.straightdope.com/t/is-there-a-god/601832/160/.

2. Jonathan Rauch, "Let It Be: Three Cheers for Apatheism," *Atlantic* (May 2003), https://www.jonathanrauch.com/jrauch_articles/apatheism_beyond_religion/index.html.

3. Jonathan Rauch, *Cross Purposes: Christianity's Broken Bargain with Democracy*, Prologue, "The Dumbest Thing I Ever Wrote" (Yale University Press, 2025).

4. Lactantius, *Divine Institutes*, Book 5, Chapter 20 (public domain), available at http://www.newadvent.org/fathers/07015.htm.

5. Dylan Thomas, "Do Not Go Gentle into That Good Night."

Conclusion

1. Jonathan Swift, *A Letter to a Young Gentleman* (1721).
2. Alexander Pope, *Essay on Man*, Epistle II, Section V.

.

Index

Browning, Robert, 84
Buckley, William F., Jr., 62
Bush, George H. W., 47

Calvin, John, and Calvinists, 117, 175
Camus, Albert, 159
cannibalism, 9, 188
capitalism, 63
capture, ideological, 6–7
Carswell, G. Harrold, 62
cheating, 3, 4, 7
checks and balances, 42–44, 46
cheerfulness, xiii, xiv, 201
Chesterton, author's cat, 112–13
Chesterton, G. K., 111, 118, 138, 151, 155, 177, 197
Christ and Christianity, 10, 118, 162, 168, 171, 174–76, 193–95
Cicero, Marcus Tullius, 105, 124
climate, 56–58
Climategate, 57–58
Clinton, Bill, 45, 47
Clinton, Hillary, 80
cohabitation, xvi, 82–85
comic books, 182
common good: belief in, 81; cherishing, 39; collectivist misunderstanding of, 36, 39; concept of often abused, 36; individualist denial of, 35; paradoxes of, 38–39; private

happiness and, 39, 138; relation to human nature, 113–14, 125; role of government in promoting, 50; senses of, 37; whether attainable through conflict, 43–44, 187
common man, 58
common sense, xiii, xx, 8, 23, 180
conscience, xviii, 19, 51, 125, 129, 187–88
consequences: causal, xv, xviii, 18, 20, 44, 65, 67–71, 75, 151, 183, 200; logical, xvii
consequentialism, 18, 20
contraceptives, 67–69, 74, 130, 200
contract, see status vs. contract
Cooper, John M., 11
Covid-19, 36, 55–56, 75

Darley, John M., 23–24
Darwin, Charles, 57, 170
Dawkins, Richard, 156, 160
de Beauvoir, Simone, 73, 124
Decalogue, see Ten Commandments
Dennett, Daniel, 160–61
design, 57, 69, 80, 107, 159–60, 170
Dillon, Meghan, 72
Dillon, Steve, 179
divorce, 80, 83–84
Donovan, Barna, 3
Dostoyevsky, Fyodor, 9, 135
Drag Queen Story Hour, xvi

❧

seem good, 133; relation to
freedom, 189; relation to grace,
49, 168, 194, 196, 198, 201–2;
relation to persecution, 192–93;
suffering and, *see* suffering;
terror of His goodness, 195–96;
Thomas Hobbes's view of, xvii;
truth about, 125, 167ff; trying to
become, 127ff; whether can be
defeated by evil, 182
Gombe Chimpanzee War, 112
Good Samaritan, 21–22
Goodall, Jane, 112
Great Barrington Declaration, 55
grifters, xv
guilt: attempt to escape, 19; formal
and material, 17; not same as
guilty feelings, 188; not same as
shame, 125

Hamilton, Alexander, 42
happiness: conditions for, 124–25;
nature of, 28–29; not same as
happy feelings, 30; not same
as satisfaction, 125; relation to
common good and, 39, 42, 138;
relation to hearth and home
and, 65; relation to limits and,
128; relation to virtue and, 27ff;
relation to wealth and, xviii–xix
harms, bodily, 10: doing for the
sake of others, 17; kinds of,

54; of so-called transitioning,
92–93; to innocents, 17; to
noncombatants, 4; weighing, 16;
what counts as, 54; while trying
to do good, 57
Harrington, Mary, 70
Harris, John, 17
Harvard University, 62
Heinrichs, Jay, 147
Henrich, Joseph, 81
Hilary of Poitiers, 186–87
Hobbes, Thomas, xvii, 154
Holden, Madeleine, 67
Hopcroft, Rosemary, 75
Hruska, Roman, 62
Hsün Tzu, *see* Xunzi (Hsün Tzu)
Hume, David, 42
Huxley, Aldous, 162

imitation and peer pressure, 8
individualism: in sense of egotism,
xviii, 36, 39, 83; individualism,
in sense of nonconformity, 62
infanticide, xvii, 11
inward-directedness, *see*
outward-directedness
Ioannis, John, 58

Jackson, Ketanji Brown, 76
John Paul II, 175
Johnson, Paul, 62

Johnson, Samuel, 65

Jordan, David Starr, 53

Judaism, 10–11, 193

just war, 4, 16–17

justice, 4, 7, 20, 30, 42, 44, 51–52, 64, 98, 112, 114, 116–17, 125, 131

Justinian's *Digests*, 4

Kahn, Shulamit, 73–74

Kurzweil, Raymond, 129

Kuyper, Abraham, 50

Lasswell, Harold, 35

Levitt, Steven D., 191

Lewinsky, Monica, 45

Lewis, C. S., 115

Lewontin, Richard, 180

lies and lying, xv, xix, 5, 31, 52, 103, 198

love, openness to, 39

Machiavelli, Niccolò, 15, 115

Mackay, Charles, xiii, 197

Madison, James, 42, 44–45

Madonna (singer), 153

Maher, Bill, xvii

Manichees, 117

markets and marketers, 58, 63, 151; *see also* economics

marriage: adulterer cannot experience the good of, 29; criticism of women seeking, 70; exuberant joy of happy, 201; lunatic views of, xvi; more than mating, 125; nature of, 79ff, 148; nonjudgmentalist view of, 185–86; recognized as a good, 10; relation to our species nature and, 104; religious teaching about, 51; view that it is impossible, 201; *see also* monogamy

Marx, Karl, 167, 195

McKie, Robin, 95

McLanahan, Sara, 80

Mead, Margaret, 11

mean, doctrine of, 30, 50–51, 54, 105

Mencius, 116

metastasis, xvii–xviii, 5, 19

moderation: false, xvi, 175; true, 105

monogamy, 9, 80–81; *see also* marriage

morality: basics of, 3ff, 189; candidates for office and, 45; derivation of, 105–6; development of, 118; development of virtues and, 21, 24, 130; disagreements concerning, 54; in relation to animals, 110–12; in relation to

fun, 28; in relation to God, 196;
in relation to human nature,
124; in relation to "moral cost,"
19; lies concerning, *see* lies
and lying; marriage and, 22;
materialist view of, 159–62;
reform of national faults and,
199; suppression of knowledge
of, 20; teaching of, 5–6, 17,
48, 51, 125; universality of,
188; *see also* evil; *see also*
excuses and rationalizations;
see also relativism; *see also* Ten
Commandments
Moses, Jennifer, 71
motivated confusion and
irrationality, 5–6, 13, 180, 189
Muggeridge, Malcolm, 165
multiverse, 181
Musk, Elon, 63, 129
Mussolini, Benito, 26
My Fair Lady, 73

Nagel, Thomas, 160, 181
narcissism, 30, 100
Nazis, 11
Neuhaus, Richard John, 2
Nietzsche, Friedrich, 143
Nixon, Richard, 62
nonjudgmentalism, 185ff

objectivity vs. neutrality, 54, 57, 177
O'Connor, Flannery, 20
Olasky, Marvin, 49
"open marriage," 82–83
outward-directedness, 77
Oxford University, 129

Page, Larry, 129
paradoxes, 38–39, 137–38, 186
Pascal, Blaise, 133, 182
Paterson, Isabel, 35
Perot, Ross, 47
persons, 35–36, 69–70, 76, 89,
99–100, 104, 151, 157
Plato, 169
polyamory, xvi, 82
Porch, Scott, 109
prediction and retrodiction, xiii,
145, 197–98
procreation, 68, 79, 80–82, 95–98
professional ethics, 7
Provine, William, 160
Puritans, 28

racism, xviii, xx, 6, 136
rationalizations, *see* excuses and
rationalizations
reincarnation, 194–95
relativism, 9–13, 143, 173, 186
republics and republicanism,
41–42, 46, 60–62, 64

wisdom: divine, 117, 175; practical, 25–26, 30
Witherspoon, John, 41
Wolfe, Gene, 92
Wright, Richard, 159

Xunzi (Hsün Tzu), 116–17

Zell, Morning Glory, 79